American
Stutter

American Stutter
2019–2021

Steve Erickson

ZEROGRAM
PRESS

ZEROGRAM PRESS
1147 El Medio Ave.
Pacific Palisades, CA 90272
Email: info@zerogrampress.com
Website: www.zerogrampress.com

Distributed by Small Press United / Independent Publishers Group
(800) 888-4741 / www.ipgbook.com

First Zerogram Press Edition 2022
This work originally appeared online in May 2021 in *Journal of the Plague
    Year*. Parts were previously published in different form in *American
    Prospect, The Believer, Los Angeles, Monkey Business*, and McSweeney's
    Small Blows Against Encroaching Totalitarianism
Book design by Creative Publishing Book Design

Publisher's Cataloging-In-Publication Data

Names: Erickson, Steve, author.
Title: American stutter : 2019-2021 / Steve Erickson.
Description: First Zerogram Press edition. | Pacific Palisades, CA :
    Zerogram Press, 2022. | Previously published in the online magazine,
    Journal of the Plague Year.
Identifiers: ISBN 9781953409102 (paperback)
Subjects: LCSH: Erickson, Steve--Diaries. | United States. President
    (2017-2021 : Trump) | Democracy--United States--21st century.
    | COVID-19 (Disease)--United States. | Wildfires--California--
    Topanga--21st century. | Divorce. | LCGFT: Diaries.
Classification: LCC PS3555.R47 Z46 2022 | DDC 813/.54--dc23

This work originally appeared in *Journal of the Plague Year*. Parts were previously published in different form in *American Prospect, The Believer, Los Angeles, Monkey Business* and *McSweeney's Small Blows Against Encroaching Totalitarianism*.

03 November 2021

I LIVE AT THE END OF one of the most famous boulevards in the world. I've been here eight months. If you told me a couple of years ago I'd be here, I'd have been astonished, but as we all know, it's been that kind of couple of years.

Anyone who comes to L.A. walks up & down this boulevard reading stars engraved in the sidewalk. I've walked it many times never supposing someday it would be my address. When I was four, my Mom & Dad brought me to the theater across the street, designed in its world-famous Chinese style, to see *Lady and the Tramp*, and even had I been old enough to ponder such things, it wouldn't have occurred to me that someday the empty window across the street would be mine. Ignorantly all of us cross, tens or hundreds of times, life's significant coordinates. All of us blithely pass places where later our lives take irrevocable turns, where later we create or destroy something of those lives. Any number of times we may stumble thru that place where we'll die. I'm old enough now that it's not out of the question this is the last place I'll live.

America wearies of democracy was the opening line of something I wrote once. One year ago today, the nation held — in the form of a presidential election — a referendum on its own nature that was inconclusive. Ten months ago, the national Capitol was pillaged in an attempted coup by thousands of domestic terrorists, killing six people & wounding scores of others. In the months since, the major political party in which I was raised means to cover up the details of this rampage so as to protect those complicit in Congress and rewrite a reality that was broadcast to the world & witnessed by billions. Virtually every state in the Union endeavors to deliver to a bankrupt Republican Party control of the counting of votes that it may then choose to reject. Last night, a series of East Coast elections politically vindicated this party's strategy with a series of bankrupt victories. Elected to numerous offices were some of the same stormtroopers of January who plundered the Capitol, and in the state that birthed the words "all men are created equal," a Black female Nobel laureate was rendered the new Willie Horton, a convicted murderer who Republicans successfully made the face of liberalism a generation ago.

All this is done in the name of no principle but power, in the name of no hope but the rest of us forgetting. It succeeds because an exhausted people allow it to. Authoritarianism abides not by instigation but inertia. More than any time in our lives, men & women of bad faith & bad conscience who have been defeated by math too often — losing seven of eight national elections in three decades — seize the only recourse left to them which is to try & defeat math back. Due process is slandered. Objective truth is subverted. Like a gasping man beneath the knee of a Minneapolis cop, democracy chokes beneath the knee of an incipient & peculiar American fascism.

If it's true that, unlike any other country, America succeeds as a grand idea, then it may be inevitable the country always has been in a state of civil war. It may be inevitable that its grand idea could never reconcile competing visions from the outset having to do with freedom & justice. In any case now that idea is cleaved more profoundly than any of us has known. Let's disabuse ourselves of the notion that the last five years were about our previous President. The last five years were about us. Donald Trump didn't happen to America; America happened to America. More than any decade since the 1860s, the 2020s will be about who we are. I began this journal two years ago at the intersection of manifesto & confession, notwithstanding fearful New York publishers advising "its ferocity stands in the way of attracting readers." Other testaments bring you facts. I come bearing the W-W-Word, stuttered but not broken.

July – December 2019

As I went out one morning
*   to breathe the air around Tom Paine*
I spied the fairest damsel
*   that ever did walk in chains*

Bob Dylan

July 03

DROP OFF MY WIFE & DAUGHTER at LAX early this morning. Viv & I adopted Zema from Ethiopia 12 yrs ago when Zema was two. Now she & Viv are going back to live five months in the land of Zema's birth, so Zema can go to school & see her birth family. It's a decision that got made almost overnight by Viv who'd argue, not altogether unfairly, that the big decisions get made by her or don't get made....

At the curb I unload the bags from the car. There are so many that there was no room for our son Parker, 21 and in his senior year at art school. So Parker & his mom & sister said their goodbyes an hour ago back at the house. Viv & I have been together 27 yrs so five months isn't so long for us, but this will be the longest time I haven't seen one of the kids. When Zema was little we called her Sheba before she insisted on reclaiming her actual birthname. Now all I can do is grab my daughter on the curb and say the name of her childhood one last time. "Sheba," I choke, "my heart hurts."

July 04

I RECEIVE AN EMAIL THAT VIV & Zema have arrived in Addis Ababa after 30-some hrs of travel, layovers, connections, customs etc....

These empty days, Independence Day is emptiest of all.

July 05

THIS IS NOT A FUCKING MEMOIR. It's not a novel, either. Everything that any reader believes to be fiction may be remembered. Everything that sounds remembered may be fiction. This is an hallucinyx. Not sure of the word's derivation but it's a real word, look it up. It means "the literary equivalent of an hallucinogen; or: the qualities of an hallucinogen reduced to literary essence…" or so says my dictionary app. Don't think you'll escape anything here. If nothing's changed by the time anyone reads this, then it's a circular journal which is to say you can begin in the middle & read to the end & then end at the beginning, a journal of scrambled page numbers or none at all….

July 06

HALLUCINYX OR NOT, I GO BACK & forth whether this is a moment for the first person. Maybe the times demand not personal impressions but a bigger picture? Along with the email from Viv, I get another from a friend that sounds for all the world like a suicide note. The fissures of the country — let's not pretend they're only fissures of politics or philosophy… these are fissures of identity — seem replicated everywhere in terms of the familial, marital, personal. Marriages implode, friendships…it's all I can do to write anything anymore, to muster any authority let alone a perspective unvarnished in a time so wrong. If I allow, I can be gripped entirely by panic

about the inevitable slipping away of family, country, mind....
In the face of an awful history to be made, I have no use for
fiction. I hasten to add I'm not talking about anyone's fiction
but mine. I hasten to add it but I don't hasten to believe it.

The story I remember most vividly of my grandmother's
dementia is the one of her waking at four in the morning
and, thinking it was four in the afternoon, wondering why it
was so dark outside. No cognitive rationale could orient itself
to any understanding other than the one on which she was
fixed — that it was four in the afternoon rather than four in
the morning, all evidence to the contrary. Now as I get older
I take afternoon naps & sleep into evening & wake thinking
I slept all night and it's early in the morning. On these occa-
sions it takes my brain what seems a long time to comprehend
where & when I am.

July 13

IN VIV & ZEMA'S ABSENCE, PARKER lives his senior college
year at home in the canyon. It's a strange bachelorhood — the
house is at once calmer & more ad hoc. News tonight that in
the coming days migrant families — most having been in this
country many years — will be rounded up & deported to...
where? Not their homelands because, legal status aside, this
is their homeland. Today the President of the United States
informs four congresswomen of color in a tweet they should
"go back where they came from." At the President's rallies,

supporters chant, "Send her back!" and not for a moment do I delude myself they aren't chanting about my daughter.

July 15

I'M INVITED TO CONTRIBUTE A PLAYLIST to an irresistibly named French radio show called *Voix de Cassandre* that broadcasts thruout Europe from England to Greece. I compile a soundtrack for a republic in freefall. This includes Johnny Cash's cover of Neil Young's "Pocahontas," Curtis Mayfield's "People Get Ready," James Brown's "Night Train," Sinatra's "I See It Now," Ellington's "Creole Love Call," Aretha's "Think," the Stooges' "Search and Destroy," Funkadelic's "One Nation Under a Groove" (single version), "This Bitter Earth" by Dinah Washington, Dave Alvin's version of "Shenandoah," "A Change is Gonna Come" by Sam Cooke.

Any place that produced all this music in a few decades must have been a hell of a country once. Music is America's contribution to the world that everyone loves however they feel about America otherwise. It's also true that all great American music is a by-product of the blues, which means a by-product of American slavery & born of an evil that the music can't redeem.

July 18

WATCHING A DOCUMENTARY TONIGHT ABOUT A young woman, smart & articulate & attractive & slightly...off, possessed or maybe crazier, who had an idea in college to invent a medical test that would — in a single drop of blood — identify any disease a human being might have. She patented her "invention," lobbied the elite of science, business & politics, caught the attention of the world. She scrambled to make her invention work before the world caught on it didn't exist. Not long ago the darling of magazine covers, now she faces prison for fraud....

I wonder whether this woman's dream was real & she believed it, or whether she did such a good job conning herself into believing it that any distinction would be without a difference. Watching her ascent & plummet, I find myself asking when does the dreamer become a zealot, when does the zealot become a con artist, when does the con artist becomes a sociopath. I recognize the obsession. I recognize the moment when belief in oneself runs off reality's rails, so all-consuming that everyone becomes its pawn. Was the madness always there? Is it a particularly American madness, like Gatsby's? Such people wind up in jail or President —

July 20

LUNCH WITH MY MOM AT A bistro on Ventura Blvd in the Valley. Up till a year ago she was 90 going on 70, remarkable, alert, energetic. Lately age catches up with her. In the last decade she has found Jesus which I guess is fair enough for someone near the end, tho she denies this is the reason. We used to talk about politics & stopped sometime around a war in Iraq that made me madder than anything till then, including the

Vietnam War for which I was draft bait. We began talking again during the intervening two terms of the previous President who she considered a socialist. Our discussions always unnerve Viv, who's never understood how our contentiousness can be so good-natured.

Since Nov 9, 2016, I'm less good-natured. I have nothing to say to my Mom and this hurts her. Today over lunch & lemon-drop martinis she finally presses me and I blurt, "Mom, it's not a matter of left and right. He's a bad guy."

"You mean he's evil?" she says, astonished.

I hedge. "For the moment I reserve 'evil' for Hitler."

"OK," she answers quietly, "but I'd rather you tell me how you feel than not talk to me." I still hold back, however, afraid I'll be overcome by fury. I can't tell her she'll be judged by history or the God to Whom she prays that I come to love Donald Trump.

July 25

THE CANYON CHOKES ON THE SMOKE of a fire 25 miles away. The cheap fabulist in me views the ashes of democracy raining down, but that would sound glib if it were my house burning. It takes no gift for melodrama to note this is the most dangerous time for American democracy in 150 yrs. The bumper sticker for the coming year isn't GET THE GUNS or BETTER HEALTH CARE but REDEEM AMERICAN DEMOCRAZY, because if we don't do that, then we do none of it. I like "redeem" better than "save" b/c it has more biblical power and, as acronyms go, I prefer RAD to SAD. Washing the dishes this morning, trying to find a sponge to clean a fork, thinking about the conversation with my Mom, I fly into rage like I haven't since the Recession when, on the verge of homelessness, one night I hurled our toaster at the kitchen wall.

July 26

OF COURSE I REALIZE MY OUTBURST yesterday wasn't about the sponge any more than the other time was about the toaster. In this time of coming apart, my country appears to be irredeemably fucked. Two & a half years into the cruelest & most corrupt administration ever, so sweeping & overwhelming is the President's depravity that it barely can be quantified. An authoritarian down to his genes, he lies publicly on an average of every 74 waking minutes. He fills the highest echelons of the government with family & cronies, an impressive number of whom have been indicted. He routinely dispenses with those for whom he's not their highest loyalty, takes credit for accomplishments he has nothing to do with, assigns blame to others for his failures. Openly & explicitly he exhorts his followers to violence. Illegally he refuses to divest his business dealings. He shields his tax records from all scrutiny, maintains shadowy ties to foreign adversaries, destroys notes & records of meetings & phone calls. He's accused of more rapes & sexual assaults than can be precisely tracked.

Born to a life of privilege, given hundreds of millions of dollars by his father that he squandered in the casino business, he's spent half a century running down the poor & powerless as "losers." He's sued contractors he stiffed, evicted African American tenants as a landlord, fired African American workers as an employer, called for the execution of African American men in full-page newspaper ads for crimes they didn't commit, mimicked & mocked the physically disabled to the laughter & cheers of supporters, and as President has stripped people of health care, deprived women of Planned Parenthood clinics, dismantled international alliances out of pique, wrecked security treaties out of jealousy for his predecessor, stacked the financial system to the benefit of the few including himself, deliberately abducted children of brown immigrants to cage them on the Texas border, and plundered the future of every child growing up on a planet perishing beneath their feet, all the while whining how unfair everyone is to him.

Now it's clear no ex machina presents itself. There's not going to be congressional removal of the President, there's not going to be a resignation in shame. There's not going to be a shortcut. We don't deserve a shortcut. We voted him in. Yes he lost the popular vote by 3 million but we all know he shouldn't have gotten within 30 million. We voted him in because on that day that's who we were and now we're going to have to vote him out because that's what we deserve. We're going to have to vote him out in a deluge massive enough not just to overwhelm vagaries, gerrymandering, voter suppression, built-in Electoral College red-state bias & interference by foreign governments but to finally wash away the bloody asterisk next to the second sentence of the Declaration of Independence placed there not by the pen but the white master's whip. On cable news tonight at a recent town hall in the Midwest, a woman stands from the crowd & cries, "If we have to have a dictator, I hope it's Trump!" and every time these past three years a Beltway commentator complains on TV that something is no longer "normal," every time someone laments the "disruption of norms," it validates disruption in the minds of those who conclude we "have to have a dictator." The voter thinks to herself, Damn straight, I didn't vote for normal. What's normal gotten me? I voted for disruption. And that voter isn't altogether wrong that only a satisfied establishment can be so vested in normal. If one believes in American Destiny then it's the nation's destiny to have gotten a President who never sees himself in the context of the country but sees the country in the context of himself.

He's not an accident. Sustained by a cult of personality & psychosis masquerading as ideology, he's revered by a third of the country not in spite of his scorn for the weak but because of it. Democracy disintegrates, the country crumbles, the world withers. What a betrayal. We've so fucked up the country, so fucked up the planet by our cavalier indices of god — greed, power, self-absorption — that surviving our kids is the only wantonness left us.

July 30

Viv & Zema have been in Addis Ababa four weeks. They've rented a house and soon Zema starts school. From the photos

I can see she's already finding herself. She had a meltdown the week after they got there & wanted to come home, but Viv put her foot down. Viv says she & I aren't so much good-cop/bad-cop as bad-cop/no-cop. I know who held the family together when Parker was 15 but it's neither here nor there. Viv was right on this & Zema flourishes.

My movie comes out month after next. Well, not my movie but one based on a novel I wrote a decade back. Last cut I saw was four years ago when they asked me to write some voice-over. Every few months since, I've dropped the filmmakers a line and they answered they were working out distribution or something, till finally they stopped responding. Then a couple days ago I read in the *Hollywood Reporter* the picture is playing at a film festival in Spain. People urge me to go. I drop an email to the director & get back an answer three hours later: *There's nobody at this email address.* Three hours seems long for an automated response, no? I suppose if the film is a failure I assume some responsibility for having sold the rights, but at the time we were the poster family for the 2008 recession — bankruptcy, massive debt, foreclosure notices, loss of two-thirds of our income, a mortgage that doubled as the house lost a third of its value.

August 06

FIFTEEN MONTHS BEFORE THE 2020 ELECTION, my heart leans to a United States Senator from my home state, a woman part black, part Asian, part progressive & part prosecutor, while my head tells my heart, Shut up, what's wrong with you, it's Joe. Polls coalesce into a godardian series of snapshots: 1) Nationally among Democratic challengers to Trump, former Vice President Biden remains a distinct but uncommanding front-runner, his appeal being he's unexciting, familiar & a respite — very vanilla after three years of Psycho Psundae with nuts & marshmallows, 2) a ménage à trois exists for second place including not only the senator from California, Kamala Harris, but fellow senators Elizabeth Warren of Massachusetts, a former Republican economics teacher, and self-avowed socialist Bernie Sanders of Vermont, 3) the only other candidate who can be called a blip is a gay former mayor of the fourth biggest city in the 17th biggest state, 4) the good & bad news for Sanders is the same, with his numbers being the most trumpian in that — relative to his previous presidential race in 2016 — they move neither up nor down, suggesting support that's both devout & stagnant, 5) on March 03, 2020 — so-called "Super Tuesday" when more than a dozen states choose their delegates — the field of more than two dozen candidates will dissolve to two or three if not produce a nominee outright, 6) the President raises grotesque amounts of money indicating a crazed core of support he's unlikely to lose, so 7) isn't it swell there are numerous articles today about Democrats deciding to run against other Democrats in otherwise safe seats b/c the incumbents aren't "progressive" enough? Exactly what the country needs right now — Democrats challenging safe Democrats. Sarandonistas of the nation, rejoice.

August 07

"Sarandonista" is a term I coined on social media where it struck a nerve, with some asking me to retire it since it's offensive to…whom, exactly? The Jeanne d'Malibu of the Resistance herself, La Sarandon? She of a far-reaching political wisdom beyond the intellectual grasp of the unwashed & shortsighted too busy worrying about kids condemned to cages in El Paso or the pregnant 18-yr-old who can't find a family clinic or the cancer patient who can't get health care or the undocumented latino family waiting in dread for ICE to rap at their door in the middle of the night or white supremacy torchlight parades in North Carolina or our daughters & sons living on a planet in flames? How small potatoes these are in the scheme of things! With a movie-star toss of her revolutionary red mane, the Sarandonista Field Marshal muses it might be better to let Trump be President than settle for left-of-center options so clearly inadequate.

To my "Sarandonista" characterization has come an outpouring of ifs, ands, buts, what-abouts, how-dare-you's, rationalizations, non-sequiturs, sleights of logic, ideological genuflecting, philosophical pretzeling in the grand tradition of stalinists selling out the Spanish Republic. "But it's your hurtful tone," sobs one demurrer. I plead guilty to my tone & every drop of it. I have ceaseless, unyielding, relentless scorn for anyone in 2016 who, practically speaking if not in fact, contributed to the current tragedy by not voting or by voting for anyone who had no realistic chance of beating the current

President. Instead of retiring the term "Sarandonista" I prefer retiring Sarandonistas themselves, and in response to that I receive messages questioning the contradiction of defending democratic values while jettisoning from my airlock into the cyber-cosmos an array of sundry dimwits & horseshit purveyors. Reasonably it's pointed out that in the United States, freedom of speech is the most cherished of rights. Check your social-media passport, however, and note that presently you're not in the United States but the Kingdom of Ericksonia where there is no Bill of Rights but a Bill of Right. It reads as follows. Amendment One: Loyal subjects of the Kingdom of Ericksonia have the right to say whatever the fuck I say they have the right to say. Amendment Two: There is no Amendment Two.

August 16

MANY YEARS AGO I HAD A friend who swore he saw in me hidden reserves of ruthlessness. He pronounced grimly that if I "ever took over, heads would roll." I scoffed. Me? I'm the original small-d democrat with tolerance for all manner of folk & viewpoints.

Of course in recent months I've come to realize my friend was right. I've gotten in touch with my inner Robespierre looking very smart in my powdered wig & bloodstained hands. Lying in bed at night when other men count harlots in private harems of the mind, I count the soulless vessels of corruption & mendacity brought before me one by one as I direct them to the large cargo plane that will drop them seven miles over the Atlantic. The jury is still out on a few, I suppose, but along with the President most are easy calls. Jim Jordan, DJTJ, Kellyanne, that Wayne LaPierre motherfucker, the Alabama legislature, oh let's not even start. When the King of Ericksonia assumes his rightful throne, these guys are done. With luck, rude atmospheric forces & raw celestial gusts will splatter them all over space before they pollute the ocean below. Number One out the door even before the gilded glob himself is the oozing Kentucky kankersore otherwise known as the Majority Leader of the United States Senate Mitch McConnell, Bile Walking Like a Man to paraphrase a Robert Johnson blues. God will never forgive me for this mass slaughter and I accept that. But She'll understand, and know I saved Her the trouble.

August 25

400ᵀᴴ ANNIVERSARY OF AFRICANS BROUGHT TO the New World in bondage…the American promise was broken before anyone knew there was a promise to break. Ultimately African Americans compelled by the genetics of freedom will dissipate our shadow in their light — if there's to be light….

The strain between Viv & me grows over the thousands of miles. My buddy Ventura visits and today we're driving around the canyon when I clip the rear-view mirror on the passenger side & send it flying off the car into the road. "You're driving angry," Ventura says.

September 02

RESENTING ALL THE ATTENTION THAT VIV & Zema's African odyssey has gotten lately from friends & family, today Parker & I decide to do something dramatic & flee a fire. This is the first time living in the canyon 20 yrs that we're forced to evacuate. I was about to have lunch in the Valley with some long-time pals when I got the call from Parker that suddenly word had come down from the fire department: *Get out.*

September 03

IT'S LESS ABOUT THE HEAT THAN the wind. Fire season comes early to California & will arrive ever earlier in the approaching years, not one fire but a phalanx to the north. Back home, loading up everything a beat-up '07 Camry could hold, I grabbed a shopping bag's worth of books, and it's interesting what choices are made in the moment of the heat: some no-brainers, my first American edition of *One Hundred Years of Solitude*, more poetry than I expected. *Dubliners* but not *Ulysses*. Because I got this particular edition in Dublin? Because it's smaller than *Ulysses* & therefore lighter? Is that a literary critique in the first couple decades of a get-ready-to-run century? Photos, some art pieces by Viv, superfluous old manuscripts that I know posterity is just dying for, and two entirely pointless dogs who displace my movie collection which I have to say I'm not OK with. I defy anyone to identify any five mins of *The Lady Eve* not worth more than both miserable animals combined. By twilight Parker & I were Flying Dutchmen of Flaming L.A., fleeing freeways like dour characters from a Joan Didion story. The silver lining of such upheaval is everyone who offers meals, places to sleep — long-time friends, short-time acquaintances, strangers on social media, ex-lovers from half a lifetime ago.

September 04

LIKE A TREE WHOSE RINGS TELL a story, a house tells a story all the more in the light of an advancing fire. It's the house where Parker lived since he was one & where Zema came to live from her Ethiopian orphanage at the age of two. It's the house I fought to save in the '09 recession, scheduled for more foreclosures than I can remember (eight? nine?). It's the house where the family was always a month away from homelessness thru '10 & '11. It's where Viv lost the flourishing career as a commercial director that bought the house, then lost the art career that began so brightly with work in exhibitions & museums. It's the house where one Sunday the morning newspaper brought an article on a new series by the world's richest artist, a series exactly like work Viv had done a decade earlier and over the ensuing months becoming a scandal in the artist's native England with headlines in the *Guardian* — DAMIEN HIRST FACES NEW PLAGIARISM ALLEGATION — & large color photos of Viv's plagiarized work. Protesters outside his galleries carried placards with Viv's name as she became the symbol of a violation by which not only her work was raped but her identity. A house can be the scene of all these things over time, lives in struggle & searches deferred.

September 08

FOR THE WEEK THAT FOLLOWS, THE family feels strewn across the planet. I take up residence in a Riverside hotel near the university where I teach. Parker is in Culver City with his girlfriend, this week Viv & Zema are in Madagascar. More than the physical scattering is a sense of no one living in concert. We each have our own individual time zones inside the world's larger time zones.

A few thousand miles away, a hurricane bears down on the East Coast following a destructive & unpredictable path. The President misspeaks in storm warnings. Hurricane Dorian heads for Alabama, he says. No it doesn't, clarifies a flustered National Weather Service. Yes it does, the President insists. Alabama collectively cries, What the fuck? As the matter becomes more nonsensical, the President's insistence becomes more adamant. In the Oval Office he pulls out maps where the storm's path has been edited by a crude black sharpie that's identifiably his even as he denies it.

September 09

EXACTLY A WEEK TO THE HOUR after having evacuated, Parker & I are back home in the canyon with our metaphysically negligible canines. A week's dislocation is a small price to pay for everyone to be safe & sound, and for having an unscathed home to return to, when so many others can't say the same.

September 14

TONIGHT A TELEVISED DEMOCRATIC DEBATE IS limited to the party's half dozen major contenders. It's been a summer of disputed hurricanes, white supremacy & Send Her Back. The question is whether Democrats understand what's at stake. To those who say, "This campaign isn't just about beating Trump," I say the hell it isn't....

More people come to support impeaching the President. Demonstrably he's sold out American national security in return for campaign dirt from Ukraine on Biden. But if impeachment is about bearing witness, then impeach him for all of it — bribery, fraud, obstruction of justice, conflict of interest, betraying his oath of office on a daily basis. If Americans give a damn about none of that, make us say so. Make it the cause of demise written on the nation's death certificate.

We all wish Bernie well but when someone has a heart attack at 78, he's not going to be President. He'll be out by Iowa.

October 28

SIX WEEKS SINCE MY LAST ENTRY. Never having met a buzz I couldn't kill, I'm sorry to say that the vote by the House of Representatives to formalize impeachment proceedings is depressing because strict partisanship means the President will be impeached, public reaction will be minimal, chances of Senate conviction are nil, and in the meantime the Republican Party out-raises Democrats in money to an almost exponential extent. *America wearies of democracy* someone wrote almost a quarter century ago — I'm sure I can't remember who. But he's still yammering in my head and I wish he'd shut up. He's never met a buzz he couldn't kill.

November 07

MARRIAGE STORY IS A MOVIE ABOUT New York nuptials hitting the skids when their union goes bicoastal. The L.A. it shows is the kind you see in pictures made by New Yorkers who think L.A. & Hollywood are the same. The L.A. where I was born & raised wasn't Hollywood but Aerospace Angeles — I played on old Western sets in the Chatsworth hills under the vapor trails of rockets tested in the Santa Susana mountains when JFK decided we were going to the moon. Ten years later that part of the Valley was porn capital of the world and that's L.A. too. Sex, Westerns & the moon share the same psychic real estate.

The movie adapted from my novel opened & closed almost literally within hours. Headline from one review: IS 'ZERO-VILLE' THE YEAR'S WORST MOVIE?

November 10

WE NEED A NEW VERB FOR what we'll hear in the coming weeks from Republicans defending the President. To *goebbels* is "to perpetuate in the public sphere so many lies so purposely brazen and audacious that they not only take a toll on the particular truths in question but on the nature of truth itself." Of course there's much different between the German Third Reich & the emerging American one, including an American tradition of democracy that Germany never had, Hitler's ability to forge a strategy & adhere to it amid growing psychosis, and a cost in human lives the Trump Administration has yet to incur.

On the other hand the most salient & unsettling similarity is the relentless assault on truth, where the President's favorite "news" network is a faithful accomplice. Republicans will goebbelize on an unprecedented scale b/c they have no other way to counter facts. We'll be told we're not hearing what we're hearing & we're not seeing what we're seeing & that things don't mean what they mean & that what's important isn't & that what isn't is. The impeachment process that Republicans argued wasn't transparent enough will be too transparent, the transcripts Republicans said we should read will be transcripts they themselves refuse to read. The question isn't whether Democrats have the goods on Trump but whether this can be communicated in a visceral way that conveys scope rather than the piecemeal. Republican goebbelizing needs to be met with truth at its plainest — more English, less latin. Stop saying *quid pro quo* and translate it into good old American bribery, blackmail & betrayal.

November 22

A WEEK THAT, EVERY YEAR, EXISTS in the crosshairs of history….A century & a half ago the most besieged President ever, under whom the country went to war against itself, made the case not only for union but its noblest requisites. It's a week haunted equally by both that declaration at the edge of a Gettysburg killing field & by the pitiless rejoinder to it almost exactly, but for a few days, 100 yrs later, an assassin's shot echoing the one that murdered Lincoln. Gunfire is the common American answer to those who call upon the country of our dreams. Of the 10 sentences constituting the entirety of Lincoln's speech at Gettysburg — following the battle there of the previous summer — eight are about the speech's inadequacy. The final two render inadequate everything that's been said or written about the speech in the years since. They're two sentences at once revolutionary & incontrovertible, transcending all ambiguity in language that's less polemic than scriptural. A hundred years & 72 hrs after the speech, the velocity of those sentences still outpaces the ballistics of an Italian Carcano rifle aimed from a high Dallas window. Lincoln's formulation now seems an obvious alignment of prepositions — so the fact that they still shock nearly as much as John Kennedy's slaughter speaks to how audacious democracy is. Of, by, for. Bang, bang, bang.

Autumn colors of bondage change to spring colors of freedom then back to autumn. Hues of one America change in the course of Lincoln's speech & then change back. Some presidencies are bigger than themselves. Lincoln's speech was bigger than his life, Kennedy's death was bigger than his. A week of anniversaries splendid & cataclysmic plays out against reminders that what's currently at stake is what Lincoln fought his war for & the terms in which he recast that war's meaning. This gave birth to the promise of the 44th President & desecration by the 45th — what's at stake are gales of martyrdom that make one President the embodiment of Lincoln's manifesto & another its defiler. On behalf of such stakes, no number of sentences is enough & one is superfluous.

December 02

PARKER, MY MOM & I WERE invited to have Thanksgiving dinner with Viv's niece & husband. The food was splendid. We spent Thanksgiving 2016 there as well, when lots of friends & family were invited and everyone was still in shock from the election….

Some people don't like her & she's been in free fall, but Kamala Harris's withdrawal from the Democratic primary is a loss.

December 10

VIV & ZEMA RETURN FROM ETHIOPIA. Earlier than usual this holiday season, tonight LAX is a mess, its circular thoroughfare clotted with cars & dashed light, a sense of motion even as barely anyone moves. New is a sense of panic.

It's the panic of people not trying to make connections but fleeing — people in flight in more ways than one. Parker & I trudge all over the airport to find the right terminal, and then suddenly Zema is in front of me and I grab her. Parker & his mom embrace and, for a moment, Viv & I breach our distance. To Viv & Zema's surprise, Parker & I kept a promise to have a Christmas tree waiting at home. Their five months in Ethiopia have been life-changing esp for Zema, but they seem glad to be back.

December 11

VIV & ZEMA SETTLE IN. After being away Viv has no patience for American politics, and today I pay as little attention as possible. Tomorrow two articles of impeachment will be presented to Congress.

December 16

TONIGHT VIV & I HAVE ONE of those fights that's ostensibly about one thing when it's really about a bigger thing. After everyone has gone to bed, I feel myself coming undone. I sleep with the light on. I've resided in my own head as long as I can remember, since before I can remember, since even the simple act of speech became a trauma, since getting the syllables out of my throat became the wracked physical effort that I still feel tighten in my chest. Now it becomes almost as much effort to write. The most natural thing I've ever done increasingly involves surmounting physical & psychic inertia. One underpinning after another feels kicked out from beneath me. I'm having a crisis of faith in all senses of the word. All my crises converge, all faithlessness converges with them — I've been in these crises awhile now and there isn't room for them in this house or family. I consider getting in the car & checking myself into an institution but that seems melodramatic. I need to find grace. I need to find a way, if nothing else, of living whatever time is left without being afraid, when at this moment I feel afraid all the time of everything. Oh, and I've got a lump in my groin. I've told no one.

December 17

THIS MORNING I ATTEND A MEMORIAL for a local reporter who took his life last week, one of those things that scrambles everyone's psychic coordinates. I met the reporter years ago when I was the subject of a newspaper profile, and the last time we saw each other, we had a public conversation before an audience at USC about Philip K. Dick. Part of me silently rages at him for what he's done to his wife & esp their small son. Another part knows he's every writer's there-but-for-the-grace-of-God nightmare. The memorial is packed in a way I suspect would have surprised him, everyone having brushed up against their own versions of his despair & wondering what sign from him we missed. He felt outside something that doesn't exist, because it's the nature of what we do & who we are to be outside.

December 18

THE PRESIDENT OF THE UNITED STATES is impeached.

Christmas Day

EVERYTHING ELSE ASIDE, CHRISTMAS IS NICE & even normal. Scheduled to fly tomorrow to Michigan to see her family, tonight Viv changes her mind. "Does Mom seem stressed to you?" Zema asks in the car.

December 28

NEWS THIS EVENING THAT CONGRESSMAN John Lewis has terminal cancer after defying death on a Selma bridge half a century ago. There aren't many men these days defined by unqualified heroism but this is one....

Begged my way into a doctor's appt rather than having to wait till after New Year's. The lump is a hernia. How, in 2019 going on 2020, can it be a hernia? How, in 2019 going on 2020, can it be anything but a plum-sized malignancy leaving me only weeks to live? I'm nonplussed. I don't believe it — it's a hoax. A hernia doesn't work for this journal at all. Surely I'm dying.

December 30

THE LETTER WAITS NEXT TO MY laptop, where I can't miss it. *I love you. I always will. I love my family absolutely and forever.*

At the same time I've changed. I know now I don't want to be part of a married couple and probably never will again. In this last chapter of my life I opt to jump into the unknown and into the possibility of actualizing my own potential rather than living someone else's life. There's more but it doesn't seem fair to share it here. Maybe even this much isn't fair.

Did you really look up *hallucinyx*? Did you actually think it's a real word & that was a real definition? This is going to be easier than I thought.

January – February 2020

The cardinal error of the Germans opposing Nazism was their failure to unite against it.

William Shirer

New Year's Day

NO NEW YEAR EVER FELT LESS like it. In the car Zema asks what my resolution is. I tell her it's to be a better Dad, but it's also not to live the year in dread.

January 03

FOR THE LAST YEAR I'VE BEEN putting together my "papers." An Ivy League university has expressed interest in an archive of my work. Part of me feels some urgency — I'm convinced they'll change their minds. "Wait, who is this guy again?" There's the tedium of collecting it all…but am I also daunted by a feeling of finality? A sense of not wanting to close the book? Growing doubt there's a book to close, growing doubt I've ever been more in danger of disappearing? Which direction swings the door of my memories — toward me or away? Is it an exit or entrance?

January 07

WHEN THE DONALD TRUMP OF THE international art scene stole Viv's work 13 yrs ago, it may have been a blow to the marriage more lethal than either of us knew. This afternoon at the Broad where an African American exhibit called *Soul of a Nation* is in its final days, a Damien Hirst book is on display in the bookstore with one of Viv's pieces on the cover. It doesn't matter that Hirst's theft became a widely documented scandal. In fact such a scandal is what makes him the Trump of artists, along with the cruelty that delights in his exploitation of someone who can do nothing about it & the shamelessness that depends on at least some of Viv's friends saying to her, "Do you really think he stole it from you?"

We don't need to spend a lot of time on this. There's a code any artist knows, a line any artist can find in the dark. She or he needs no rulebook, no need for a seminar or round-table discussion. The artist understands the difference between theft & sway b/c *author* is the root word of *authority* — he knows the malevolence that distinguishes what's influenced from what's purloined. If you're going to steal, steal up. Steal from Monet, Chagall, Warhol. Don't be the world's richest artist stealing from a lesser-known artist on the other side of the planet figuring nobody will notice, assuming you care. Can I write something here that would bait him into suing me? Is there anything that won't add to the naughty-boy image he loves? Is "parasite" unglamorous enough? Leech? Maggot? Or is *trump* worse than all of them?

January 18

VIV & I VISIT AN AFRICAN American bookstore in Leimert Park. No Damien Hirst books here. I pick up a biography of Frederick Douglass who, other than Lincoln, was as important as any American of his century — no one more influenced the American promise. There's a play to be written about the

times these two men crossed paths not without misgivings &
contentiousness, with Douglass impressing Lincoln as the most
remarkable man he ever met & Lincoln impressing Douglass
as the only white man who treated him as his equal.

2020 will be a year whose history is so monumental we can't
now know its ramifications any more than people in 1864 knew
the ramifications of 1864. Not only can anyone be excused for
believing everything is on the line, anyone who doesn't believe
it is a chump. The President could vanish into thin air & there
still would be trumpism. This cold civil war is going to rage
another generation & we need to hunker down, stock up on
provisions, conceive strategies. Draw up battle plans & don't
spare the ammunition. An anthem wouldn't kill us either. I'll
bring my Scandinavian death-metal keyboard, the one attached
to this laptop. Nobody does despair like Scandinavians, who
have rock bands called Autopsy Torment and Slaughter of the
Soul. We make movies about playing chess with Death, except
any real Scandinavian who won would demand a rematch.

January 26

SANDERS IS POSITIONED TO WIN CAUCUSES & primaries
in Iowa, New Hampshire & Nevada. I remember someone
writing a while back that Bernie wouldn't make it to Iowa
after his heart attack. Boy, if I ever said anything that stupid,
I'd never open my mouth again.

Parker & Zema are Berniacs. Assuming Sanders is still
in the race on Super Tuesday, Parker will vote for him. Zema

has a handmade sign on her bedroom door with a picture of Sanders that warns THOU MUST FEEL THY BERN TO COME FURTHER.

January 28

CANT SLEEP READS AN OLD NOTE I find in Zema's room that she wrote to herself years ago. *I feel like no one cares about me sometimes. life is ok I guess but Dad does not under stand me.* Parenthood is an ongoing lesson in what a clueless father I am & a clueless white liberal on top of it. Back around the Ferguson shootings five years ago, people talked of "the Talk" parents have with their black children — about racism & police & where to put your hands on the steering wheel if you're pulled over & how black people should never run in public b/c just the act of running to catch a bus will be viewed with fear & suspicion. What's she running from? Who's she running after? These days I don't have the talk with Zema — rather Zema has the talk with me. The rare moment when she says anything in the car on the way to school, I turn down the music to listen. "Brown Sugar" by the Stones, as it happens.

January 29

I FIRST HEARD IT IN COLLEGE. One of my half-dozen favorite Rolling Stones songs...I loved it even as the lyrics sank in. Actually that's a lie. I'm a liar if I don't admit the lyrics were part of the song's attraction just as they're part of the attraction of "Stray Cat" & "Parachute Woman" & "Backstreet Girl." The Stones' function was to harvest forbidden fruit & run the X-ticket rides in the amusement park of the mind. Fast forward several decades to being Zema's Dad & then another to living under a presidency that stokes white supremacism and suddenly "Brown Sugar" makes me uncomfortable in a way I always had the luxury of ignoring. Going on 15, Zema is smart enough to understand "Brown Sugar" means to be a commentary on racism, and she's also smart enough to know this argument doesn't fly in these debased times.

A year ago I was teaching a seminar when, as fate would have it, I assigned Nabokov's *Lolita* just as the scandal broke involving child sex-trafficker Jeffrey Epstein. I made clear to the students they were free to hate or love the novel on any terms they chose — I've always considered *Lolita* an object lesson in literary duplicity by an author who knew better. If a middle-aged writer/professor writes a novel about a middle-aged writer/professor with molestation in his heart, at least engage the material without tricks & jokes. There's a reason Nabokov threw the book in a fire after working on it five years, only for Ms. N's nimble fingers to snatch it from the flames....

The Trump era is a minefield even for the culturally unimpeachable. African American crime writer Walter Mosley is admonished by a human resources department on a TV show for using the n-word in a conversation that quotes a racist cop, and having put up with racism his whole life Mosley reasonably determines he doesn't need lectures from corporately discomfited white folks. Language exists in a context. African Americans have earned the right to gauge the word's validity in the context of their own usage, but from the mouth of a white person that same word has no context that matters more than 400 yrs of bad bad shit. So on the one hand it's absurd that a white teacher nearly loses her job for quoting James Baldwin verbatim & on the other hand any white person is naïve to think none of that word's shrapnel is going to boomerang in the way it did on Mosley who's not even white —

Notwithstanding the Bill of Rights & Lincoln's second inaugural & Martin Luther King's 1963 speech at the Lincoln Memorial, there's no user's manual for America. If the President were to replace "You Can't Always Get What You Want" at his rallies with "Brown Sugar," it wouldn't change the song as the Stones wrote & played it, but there's also no way it wouldn't change what the song means to those hearing it. No one can doubt that those in charge politically — as white & male as I — exploit this confusion. No one can doubt they love the way we hate each other, b/c that's what puts them in charge & keeps them there. No one can question the right of anyone to write or read *Lolita*, and no one can question the right of anyone to be offended by it & say so. None of this is contradictory. Truth validates rather than negates other contending truths.

These are complications that ideologues of both Right & Left resent. A sanitized culture always on its good behavior & bleached of provocation is no culture at all. It's a garden party where no one talks of anything but the weather, and these days even the weather is controversial. In America, culture defines politics rather than the other way around. It remains to be seen whether the culture wrests back from our times the courage of disquieting provocations....

February 02

DROPPING "BROWN SUGAR" FROM MY PLAYLIST for the duration of this presidency. Keith's opening riff is yet another reason to vote Trump out. After that, it's a matter to be settled by black daughters & white dads in the call & response of their consciences. But at this moment I find it impossible to love both my daughter & the song.

February 04

THE IOWA CAUCUS IS ALL FUCKED up with no declared winner...exit polls indicate former South Bend Mayor Pete Buttigieg narrowly beating Sanders, who got half the vote that he got in the 2016 Iowa contest when he lost to Hillary Clinton. Biden's concession speech has people holding their heads in despair. More unsettling is the flat participation compared to the massive turnout of the 2018 midterms just 15 months ago, when 9 million more Americans voted Democrat than Republican.

February 06

THE PRESIDENT IS ACQUITTED BY THE Senate.

February 07

FREAKISH DOWNPOUR OF HARD HAIL THIS morning
in the canyon. Two days after both his Senate acquittal &
another dismal debate by Democratic presidential candidates,
the President's poll numbers are up as he fires all the witnesses
who testified in the impeachment hearings. Sanders is now
Democratic frontrunner even as his support shrinks from what
it was four years ago. Biden's aspirations appear all but done
even as he remains the only Democrat who appeals to African
Americans, working-class whites, moderates, independents,
white suburban women. Republican turnout grows for Trump
in primaries where he's unopposed, his base revved & ready
to come out for him in full & frenzied force....

In leather & stiletto heels, God comes to me in one of my
dreams where I guess She hangs out. "I've been reading your
stuff posted in My third Ring of Hell otherwise known as
Facebook," She says, "and also the responses to them, some of
which are reasoned and bear some sense of moral proportion,
and many of which are addled, deranged or just silly, for which
I hold you responsible." Naturally I ask, "Wait, how am I
responsible?" and She answers, "Because that's the way it works,
haven't you read the testaments? I never punish the guilty. I
punish the innocent in order to make a point to the guilty. Ask
Isaac. Ask Job. Ask Jesus. Ask Egypt's first-born sons." Then
She takes me back to Berlin in early 1933 and we're standing
on the Unter den Linden near the Brandenburg Gate like in
a tourist photo. She says, "Now you have a choice to make.

The fate of the world is in your hands. Von Hindenburg or Hitler? with the understanding that Hitler is the default here if you don't choose." I say, "A little hypothetical, wouldn't You agree?" and with a thrilling crack of her whip She snaps, "It's better than hypothetical — it's capricious. That's what proves I'm God."

Having read the responses to something I recently posted & subsequently seen the light, I confidently explain, "Now 24 hours ago this would have been an easy decision, but since then I've seen the light. Since then I've come to realize I'm just way too morally superior to choose between an aging moderate warmed-over hack — not altogether unlike Biden — who will perpetuate a broken Weimar, and a psychotic megalomaniac who will plunge the world into darkness and death. They're both essentially the same thing, both just as bad, two sides of the same coin if you will and, well, we'd just be settling for the lesser of two evils."

God nods, "Yeah, that's what I figured you'd say, which is why you get the history you do for as long as it lasts, which won't be much longer. Hey," and here She can't help bursting into laughter, "ever notice how the Sarandonistas never post anything about Trump that's half as incensed as what they post about Hillary or Biden or even Obama or, basically, anyone but Bernie?" and I explain, "That's because they recognize — from their elevated peak on the mountaintop of human perspective — that various impurities of the Resistance to Trump are worse than Trump himself. No better, anyway," and God slaps Her forehead with Her hand & mutters something I can't make out. "What?" I ask.

"Read the next line," She says.

"Read — ?"

"…the…next…line."

February 08

…AND I WAKE ON THIS SIDE of midnight to read the next line on page 259 of the 1,400-pg book open in my lap: *The cardinal error of the Germans who opposed Nazism was their failure to unite against it.*

February 17

HEADLINES THIS MORNING ABOUT A "BUOYANT" Trump. Of course he's buoyant. Acquitted of patently impeachable offenses, he runs against Democrats who talk more about each other than about him.

Five presidential elections in our history where the Electoral College winner lost the popular vote…in four cases the election was razor close. Even setting aside 2000's controversy about a shambolic Florida recount & the Supreme Court decision that "resolved" it, George Bush lost the popular vote by only half a percent & received 271 electoral votes, exactly one more than needed — which is to say the popular & electoral results each reflected the other's narrow edge. In 2016 Trump lost the popular vote by nearly 3 million & won the Electoral College by 80. We've never had that kind of disparity. He did it by surgically amassing one quarter of one percent of the total in precisely the right districts in precisely the right states.

In the fall of 2016 I posted on social media the question, "Is anyone still paying attention?" While friends know I'm prone to outbursts of nordic hysteria, the question was prompted by how Trump was being written off when polls showed he was very much in the race. There's an urban legend that the 2016 polls were wrong, but except for a moment after the release of a tape on which Trump bragged about accosting with impunity whatever woman he wanted, national surveys consistently showed Trump within single digits of victory. Regardless the Democratic mindset remained that Trump was unelectable right up to the moment that many stayed home & elected him.

February 19

IS ANYONE STILL PAYING ATTENTION? EVERYONE whistles past their favorite graveyards. The economy slows with farming & manufacturing suffering the brunt and stories grow of a strange virus out of China. Americans of both parties have gone from believing the President is a buffoon who could never win to believing he's an evil genius who's invincible. A third of the country constitutes the Fifth Avenue Columnists who align with the President to the bitter end no matter who he shoots on Fifth Avenue, while another segment of the country believes people stupid enough to be fooled by him make him smarter than he is. Half the country makes clear they won't vote to reelect Trump under any circumstances. Nonetheless it remains within Democrats' capacity to lose if they indulge in anything like the thinking that characterizes Trump supporters, so vested in their cult that the worse he does, the more vested they become.

I began having my sinking feeling about Trump in spring 2016. Parker went to a party & noted the Bernie kids had more in common with the Trump kids than with the Hillary kids, and if this was anecdotal, nevertheless something about it rang ominously true. People who pay little attention to politics in general, which is to say most Americans, pay even less attention to ideology, which is how 2008 Obama voters could vote for Trump in 2016 — the insider/outsider divide counts for more than left/right. Trump is a rorschach: Where the rest of us see a blot of shit, his supporters see a bird or bunny.

Several developments unfold in the foreseeable future. We become a country of minorities & no majority, alarming an aging white populace. We become a country where the racially mixed majority lives in 15 states represented by 30 senators while the dying white minority lives in 35 states represented by 70 senators — the identity of the Republic goes one way as its politics go the other, with representational democracy collapsing between them. More power & wealth accrue to a ruling elite at the expense of everyone else. In the face of that, someone who has been out of work 10 yrs & on the verge of losing his house to globalization sees a vote for white power as a desperate Hail Mary in a country where tens of millions of white Americans still won't admit a century & a half later that the Civil War was about slavery — the American version of Holocaust denial. You don't need to be an atheist (I'm not) or a secularist (I am) to know faith in objective truth is the bulwark that holds back the forces of darkness.

The President is an extravagant iteration of 1990s Republican Speaker of the House Newt Gingrich and '50s Senator Joe McCarthy before him, their common modus operandi being to deliberately toxify American politics & plumb its depths. For a quarter century before it found the face & claimed the name of Trump, the Republican Party moved both relentlessly & glacially toward an exquisitely calibrated hatred of the American Promise — a hatred canny enough to brand itself patriotism. True to the cliché, over the past half century Republicans successfully branded Democrats in cultural terms of sex, drugs, abortion, immigration & overseas humiliation, and time & again generations of working-class whites were thereby persuaded to vote against their economic interests. Now Republicans successfully brand Sanders, Warren & new congressional star Alexandria Ocasio-Cortez as radicals & disassociate them from economic positions with which most people otherwise agree. If the victorious candidate in a general election is the one who successfully makes the other candidate the issue, then the needle that any nominee must thread is at once mobilizing the base & winning the middle. Only two people in the last half century, Obama & Ronald Reagan, have done this with any resounding consistency. Any Democratic nominee who enters the fall campaign defending his or her radicalism without a united party is a loser.

February 20

REFLECTING (IF THAT'S THE WORD) ON comments made in the recent Democratic debate, and inspired (if that's the word) by responses on social media, I ponder the woman who can't catch a break. Her name is Hillary Clinton and it's taken in vain these days on the Left as well as the Right. As an Obama supporter in 2008, I feel bound nonetheless to point out that Hillary edged him in the primaries by 200k votes & lost the nomination anyway. Then she beat Trump by nearly 3 million votes & lost the presidency anyway. Now Sanders supporters bitterly insist she stole the 2016 nomination from a man she beat nationally in the primaries by 4 million votes, more than her margins over Obama & Trump combined. When did the empiricism of math get so amorphous? God knows sexism & misogyny have nothing to do with it, right? Whatever her shortcomings as a candidate, she was a brilliant & dedicated public servant who doesn't deserve revisionist slander. History will accredit what liars have denied her....

Some may argue straight-faced there's no difference between a flawed Democratic Party & an increasingly neofascist Republican Party, but with a primary in South Carolina looming, I suspect African Americans see a difference. I suspect immigrants see a difference. Patients without health care see a difference, those serious about saving the planet see a difference. The Democratic primary voter who can't or won't understand that this year's election involves not mere matters of policy but a momentous historic choice has a roulette wheel for a moral compass. None of this is to deny Sanders's arguments. It doesn't take a socialist to figure out that, since the waning years of the 20th century, capitalism isn't working. Greed sells out the fate of entire species including our own — free-market genocide. During the '08 recession when unrestrained capitalism drove the world economy off a cliff, on the verge of losing our house & with credit debt in the low six figures I used to lie on my bed & calculate how much my family might collect on my life insurance if I could just find a way to be dead. Privatization of health care doesn't work because a national economy can't sustain the avarice of those who make money on the sick & dying. Sanders is right about health care. He's right about the insurance companies. He's right about the banks. He's right about Wall Street. He's right about the very wealthy, three quarters of whom inherit their money rather than earn it.

The only thing he's wrong about is the electorate. Sanders will spend months explaining "socialism" to four states in the industrial Midwest that have a million fewer voters than California but nine more votes in the Electoral College. Medicare for All is a stone loser. It's taken 10 yrs for Obamacare to become popular after Democrats paid a political price to enact it, so by all means let's toss it aside as not radical enough in order that Democrats can spend another 10 yrs losing elections. Say, has anyone heard about this President we have now? Is anyone still paying attention? He's not a "conservative," he's not even a right-winger, b/c that would involve principles. He's a sociopath with authoritarian tendencies that, like his supporters, aren't partisan but pathological. If he wins reelection, it won't matter which Democrat had the better health care plan, it won't matter who had the better climate-change plan or the better plan for student debt. For a while I couldn't understand why some couldn't grasp this till I realized they don't want to. It pleases their neuroses — in the way Trump pleases the neuroses of his supporters — to believe there's no difference between Trump & any Democratic candidate except Bernie. It's "idealism" disguising vanity disguising complicity.

You would think a truly progressive base might find four more years of Trump motivating enough. In the face of trumpism, however, Democrats focus their ire not on Trump but other Democrats. Vexed by the inconvenience of math — by which the more members of Congress there are with D's next to their names, whatever their ideological shadings, then the more that Democrats control the national agenda, the more that Democrats control congressional committees, the more judges they appoint — some progressives dismiss it altogether. Senator Joe Manchin of West Virginia may be an asshole — he's also the only kind of Democrat who's going to win in a state like West Virginia, and if Democrats are going to take the Senate & depose the rot that calls itself Mitch McConnell, they must reconcile themselves to the political realities of West Virginia at least when it comes to West Virginia. Instead Democrats become a party where every candidate on a debate stage reflexively raises his or her hand when asked who favors free health care for people here illegally, which you don't need to be a right-wing racist to know makes no sense. It's no different than Republicans reflexively raising their hands in debates on behalf of capital punishment & abortion bans & arming every 11-yr-old with an automatic. Democrats overreact to everything & Republicans underreact to anything. The result is Democrats getting Republicans reelected who then further doom immigration reform, health care, higher education, economic fairness, the planet —

I like Ocasio-Cortez. I'd like her more if she had taken a Republican seat instead of a safe Democratic one. I like Warren too & would like her more if she complained about Trump instead of Obama. Warren already struggles to get traction with African American voters so she might be well advised to call a truce damn quick with the second most popular person in the country after his wife. Too often on the Left as well as the Right, too many people in 2016 chose to believe every terrible thing they heard about Hillary while disregarding every terrible thing we knew about Trump. On the lives of my kids I have more contempt for Sarandonistas who won't make the best of clear if imperfect binary choices than I do for the unemployed Michigan father of two who voted for Trump in an ill-considered act of desperation. Objections are raised to

Biden as a "restoration candidate" because, it's argued by some, 2016 wasn't that hot and who'd want to restore it? Taking all things into account, I suggest here as tactfully as possible that anyone who doesn't think 2016 was better than 2020 is… how to put it? employing precise language that contributes to a general elevation of the national discussion…the stupidest fucking person on earth. "Electability" has become a dirty word in progressive conversations. It's taken as code for white guys when in fact this year it's code for African American guys & suburban white women who didn't turn out last time. The contention that electability is a specious argument is made on behalf of candidates for whom no electability argument can be made in the first place.

February 22

DISMAYING AS IT MAY BE, THE candidate with the best chance of beating Trump remains Biden with his baggage of age, Anita Hill, curious bouts of plagiarism & gaffery run amok. In terms of policy, likely he'll move left on Obamacare and, if he can, on some reinstatement of a more progressive tax rate that created in the 1950s, under wild-eyed bolshevik Dwight Eisenhower, the greatest standard of living the world has seen before or since. Biden's appeal is nothing more than to a gnawing roiling collective craving for someone just a little decent, just a little experienced, just a little old-school, just a little dull enough not to brag about grabbing pussy. I've never been a Biden supporter in his other presidential runs and I was disappointed when Obama picked him in '08 for Vice-President tho I accepted the reasoning. I was opposed to Biden running in '16 b/c I thought it was Hillary's time. If I could put anyone in the White House, I'm not sure who it would be but probably not Biden. But for as long as he's best poised of the Democrats to win the national election, that's all…I…care about. I don't care who has the purest past, I don't care who has the best position on health care or any other indisputably important issue. I don't give a frack who has the best position on fracking. I care about who's in the best position to save democracy. It's that simple. I'm the world's least complicated man.

February 24

WELL, BERNIE'S GOING TO BE THE Democratic nominee just like I've been saying. OK, I haven't exactly been saying that. OK, I haven't been saying anything like that. The problem is that the turnout so far producing his victories is down, not up. Beginning to pop to the surface are Sanders stories bubbling under for years having to do with guns, taxes, Soviet honeymoons. Protest tho the Berniacs may, this isn't a corporate conspiracy, it's the name of the game — front-runnership — like the email server was for Hillary in 2016 & like preacher Jeremiah Wright was for Barack in '08 & like half the women in Arkansas claiming to have fucked Bill Clinton in 1992.….

South Carolina Primary is in two days, Super Tuesday in five. Best news of the Democratic primary so far are indications of a turnout in South Carolina nearing 2008 levels. I've narrowed my vote to Biden or Warren.

February 28

IF EVER THERE WAS AN ELECTION where I'm disinclined to throw my vote away, it's this one. Biden reassures everyone & excites no one. He's an uneven candidate at best, poor at worst. A Ukrainian controversy involving his son has never looked great however innocent Hunter Biden may be. But so far Joe is the only Democrat competitive against Trump. He has to win the South Carolina Primary tomorrow. If by some chance he were to do so commandingly, his campaign might be back on track & in a position to run second on Super Tuesday....

Warren has a reputation as the smartest candidate in the race b/c she is. She knows pragmatism has its place if you want to accomplish anything, and that she was a Republican in a previous life is as much a plus as a minus. Best about her: She fights. Down & out at least a couple times over the year, nevertheless she persists, as Mitch McConnell once put it, and does so in the face of a sexism on both Right & Left that takes her to task for not spelling out more specifically a health-care plan that Sanders gets away with not even putting a price tag on. Warren never says die. As nominee & President she would be Persister-in-Chief. Her campaign, however, is a knotty mass of wonky dispositions in search of a vision or at least the expression of one. I can only suppose her displeasure with other Democrats in recent debates has meant to serve as an audition for taking on Trump, in which case a better audition might have been taking on Trump. Warren hasn't done better than fourth in a major contest so far & she's fourth in national polls. She's not going to be the nominee.

In a spirit of full disclosure, can I add one more thing? I have no idea what the fuck I'm talking about. I thought Bernie's heart attack was the end when in retrospect it galvanized a campaign that was static — tho I don't think Sanders wants to tempt the gods with so much as a flu let alone some weird asian "coronavirus."

Leap Day

SOME ON SOCIAL MEDIA TELL ME to "get off [my] high horse," always valid advice in my case. But will this journal wind up a chronicle of resurrection or self-immolation? More often than readers realize — wait, let me climb a little higher on my horse for this — authors don't always know how their stories turn out. Countries don't know how their stories turn out even on the final page. Electing Hitler as Chancellor with not much less (40%) than Trump got in 2016 & sharing collective contempt for the Weimar, Germans went into full swoon for the shiny new futurism he built them right out of a Fritz Lang movie, and who bothered about that little matter of Jews & Slavs vanishing in the night? But seven years later the only enthusiasts for Hitler's war were Hitler himself & right-hand hatchet man Göring. The Devil always shows up at the wedding late, when everyone thinks the ceremony is over. After he does, the marriage is never the same. Temptations have been flirted, seductions made, irrevocable deals involving the soul are struck with no option of unstriking them....

Most people assume that, in the Bible, the Devil is the snake in the Garden. Actually the Devil's first appearance is around Chronicles, the two books that sum up the Old Testament. While it wouldn't be accurate to say the Devil is an invention of Christianity, it would be fair to suggest he doesn't have the swagger for Jews that he has for Christians. As Christians have revised Jesus over millennia from the obscure figure in Mark to the forgiving one in Matthew to the son of a bitch in John that all the evangelicals love, the Devil has become more charismatic as well & even more subject than Jesus to interpretation. Sometimes he's an abstraction who's more chaos than evil. Sometimes he's a con man, sometimes he's a fallen angel pitted against a God to whom he's equal or close to it. In a 20th Century of holocaust & annihilation, the Devil of mass popular culture took on the incarnation of the damned & irredeemable, the persona given to whatever absolute we call Evil. The paradox is that the more absolute something is, the more subjective — which is to say the Devil remains in the eye of the beholder or, as the case may be, the producer of a miniseries on the History Channel.

Pressed to offer an American Satan, I might go with Nathan Bedford Forrest, the sadistic Confederate war criminal who murdered slaves & started the Ku Klux Klan, and in whose honor more statues dot the present-day South than for all the presidents combined. But the hooded figure slogging thru the African sands in the 2013 TV saga *The Bible* doesn't look anything like Forrest. Rather he looks exactly like Barack Obama.

Other than one's lying eyes, there were few reasons to doubt *The Bible*'s producers when they insisted the resemblance between Obama & Mehdi Ouazanni, the Moroccan Islamic actor playing Satan, was entirely coincidental. Out of all the actors in all the gin joints, apparently Ouazanni was chosen b/c it's a role he played in the past — peculiar type-casting. The resemblance between Obama & Ouazanni was first noted not by paranoid leftists but conservative TV huckster Glenn Beck, who always made a point of never voicing Obama's name in the manner of Hogwarts wizards never voicing Voldemort's. Other professional blabbermouths of the Right advised that while the producers didn't mean to make Satan look like Obama, God guided the hand of the series' makeup artist & blinded everyone on the set.

Christians have a love-hate relationship with Satan. They're nowhere without him. The more God-fearing you are, the more useful the Devil is, till a point is reached when the Devil is more useful than God. During the Obama presidency, Republicans considered any association with Obama so ghastly that some congressmen opposed bills bearing their own names just to avoid the sulfuric whiff of presidential support. Having abandoned everything but a perfunctory semblance of principles, the Republican Party was a cult of personality before Trump ever came along — it just so happened to be Obama's personality. When a church's devil comes to mean more than its jesus, the quest is no longer about deliverance but damnation....

Parker had just turned 15 when Sandy Hook happened. Zema was seven. Viv was back in Michigan seeing her family and I was a single dad. When the news broke, I remember Obama came on the TV over the bar in the restaurant where I sat and some of the waiters stopped to watch. Obama brushed something from one eye & only when he brushed the other eye did I know for sure this was something I hadn't seen before. Later when he spoke at a memorial service in Newtown, interrupting a televised football game & enraging sports fans, he was more composed at first, his emotions threatening to overwhelm him only near the end when he recited the names of the 20 murdered kids younger than Zema was. He had just met with their families in a congregation that we have to imagine exhausted whatever vocabulary of grief can possibly suffice for such a moment. Any parent who had a seven-year-old knew that the brave declarations made that night — by the President & the state's Governor & various clergy — to endure what happened & somehow prevail were a lie. I'm not suggesting anything different should have been said. I just mean that any parent knows Sandy Hook was something no parent survives in any condition that isn't forever broken. This was no wound that time or anything else heals. I imagine the best you're able to do in such circumstances is recreate some fractured version of what your life was before & hold it together with the adhesive of some new commitment. But that crack in your life isn't going away.

Obama said that night what any reasonable person was thinking, even if the points made by those who love their guns so much are conceded. We can concede that curtailing the state's power to disarm the citizenry is important & that's why the second amendment to the Constitution exists. We can concede that the deranged will find ways to express their derangement whether they have guns or not. We can concede that a ban on certain kinds of weapons may not prevent a massacre. We can concede that the suppression of guns will create a black market for them. We can concede a violence in the American DNA that doesn't manifest itself in, say, a similarly armed Canada. We can concede all that & still be left with the question of what point a nation has to reach to make a statement on behalf of its own civility. At what point do we take responsibility for our national character by doing something b/c it's right & we have blood on our hands? After Sandy Hook you sensed something snapped in the country. You sensed something snapped in all of us, or most of us anyway — you heard the snap in yourself that surely this was the tragedy too far, these were the 20 small lives too many, not to mention the six teachers who tried to protect those kids. Surely it was, until it wasn't.

Now four years post-Obama, in this crucial year of the Donald Trump presidency, several "progressive" "news" outfits have decided this is the perfect political moment to publish pieces about how short of perfection Obama fell. At the moment that Obamacare was passing the Senate 10 yrs ago, I was being verbally abused about it on a plane flight by the stranger seated next to me who noted over my shoulder the trotskyite reading matter — CNN — on my laptop. "The difference between us," she informed me, "is I'm a responsible person and you're not," and I suppressed the question of whether she had children, b/c I sensed she didn't and that, of a certain age, she never would, and I couldn't bring myself to land that cruel a blow. Conveniently forgetting what went into passing this compromised health-care reform, the latest "reportage" is the same Sarandonista sleight-of-logic that helped elect Trump in the first place. Why in the fourth year of an authoritarian administration are so-called progressives wasting one word let alone thousands on Obama, who only put his presidency on the line to try & pass gun reform, to pass the first major health-care reform since Medicare, to avert a worldwide economic Chernobyl, to rescue the auto industry, to create more jobs in three years of recession than in the previous administration's eight or the succeeding administration's four, to advance gay rights, to protect women in the workplace & sign a law codifying equal pay for equal work, to denuclearize Iran while decimating the terrorist organization that murdered 3k Americans on 9/11, and to speak on a weekly if not daily basis to our better angels? Not having done it all fast or fully or elegantly enough, yes, Obama was just as bad as Trump.

Obama's greatest failure was living up to his metaphor. It's the nature of politics that metaphors are lived down to. For his supporters Obama failed to be in the best sense the transformational figure that his opponents accused him of being in the worst sense. By the alignment of temperament, talent & timing that got him elected him in 2008, he personified the country's contradictions including both an aspiration to redemption & the failure to come to grips with 400-yr sins. What the Right found radical about Obama wasn't anything he said or did. In terms of policy, not only Lyndon Johnson but Harry Truman was more progressive. What the Right found radical about Obama was the fact of him.

Obama's presidency itself was a transgression to Americans who believe things started going very wrong in this country sometime around 1861. Our response to Obama was the national psychotic break that Trump embodies. On Left & Right we made Obama our metaphor in the face of anything he actually said or did, we were rendered hysterical by a presidency that existed both in spite of metaphors & because of them. Hysteria in favor of Obama upon his election — as unsustainable by the public as it was by Obama himself — gave way within weeks of his inauguration to counter-hysteria suggesting he was the passport-snatching spawn of African veldts. This was the enraged response to a euphoria too uncommon to last any longer than fleetingly.

None of the hostility to Obama was about "conservatism," a term changing more profoundly than the term "socialism." Rejected in his 1964 presidential run as the most far-right nominee of the post-World War II era, the so-called "Mr. Conservative" Barry Goldwater favored voting rights, abortion rights, gay rights, Native-American rights & protecting the environment, and spent the last decade of his life unambiguously (pretty much everything Goldwater did was unambiguous) detesting the theocratic impulse that in the '80s characterized a Republican

Party significantly to the left of the party today. Ideology shapeshifts to fit pathology masquerading as philosophy. Unlike the Reagan Right before or the Trump Right after, an Obama Right was defined not by its jesus but by its devil regardless of how this devil bore no resemblance to anyone except Mehdi Ouazanni. What increasingly constitutes the incipient fascist heart of the Trump Right is enmity to the truth of weather patterns & people changing them, the truth of women getting pregnant when they're raped, the truth of a Constitution that never mentions or alludes to God or Jesus or capitalism, and the truth of someone like Obama being President.

In news tonight, the primary results begin coming in from South Carolina where they do at least one thing sensibly & vote on Saturday. Meanwhile, what's the deal with this asian flu? If there's a God, is it a plague sent as an Old Testament punishment of the Pharaoh Donald?

March – April 2020

The ideal subject of totalitarian rule is people for whom the distinction between fact and fiction, between true and false, no longer exists.

Hannah Arendt

March 01

BIDEN HAS WON HUGE IN SOUTH CAROLINA & saved his candidacy. African Americans went to the mat for him. In all the primary contests thus far combined, Biden now has more total votes than any candidate. Sanders remains the frontrunner, maintaining a slim delegate lead, and is poised to win day after tomorrow on Super Tuesday. Meanwhile I have to figure out my Super Tuesday vote....

Super Tuesday

IT'S STRANGE TO HAVE STARTED OUT with Biden eight months ago while flirting with other possibilities from Harris to Warren only to end up back at Joe, to whom my head has been faithful as the heart has wandered. In other words I've been an electoral slut ready to sleep with any of them, Barbara Stanwyck to any Fred MacMurray who'll just climb in my backseat & smash Donald Trump's fucking head in at the signal of the honked horn, with me all orgasmic in closeup. After months of Joe's botched debates & lackluster performance, as of this morning's polls he still runs better than any Democrat against Trump, and I'm still having a hard time coming up with more than a dozen states that Sanders has any chance of winning in the best circumstances. And now that you've taken another look, Biden is a stone-noir killer if you've ever seen one, am I right? Shades, slicked back hair, even the name is right out of Cain. Honk the horn & let him have it, Joe.

March 05

BLOWOUT. ENTIRELY UNFORESEEN, BIDEN HAS SWEPT 10 states of 14 including some where he didn't spend five mins campaigning. Six days of frontrunner scrutiny on Sanders appear to have taken some toll. Warren is out. I didn't vote for her but I'm sorry to see her go.

March 07

TERRENCE MALICK'S *A HIDDEN LIFE* IS the true story of an Austrian farmer who wouldn't swear loyalty to Hitler even as his refusal had no potential of changing anything. One of the agonies watching the movie is how we, the audience, keep trying to find a way out for him. We keep trying to get him off a hook that he won't let himself off, when a hastily & inconsequentially scribbled signature on a piece of paper will save his life. Just sign it, for God's sake! we silently plead. With his hushed murmurs Malick forgives us — dread rising from rapture, the collapse of sense before the majesty of an MIA god....

We shouldn't be too glib in our comparisons of what's going on in this country now with what went on in Europe in the '30s. It cheapens the consequences. But besides the exaltation of cruelty & pitilessness as "virtues" that render more human virtues contemptible, constants of fascism include a cult of personality in which people surrender sense & rationale to a single charismatic figure; the abdication of truth & an acquiescence to lies that, in their temerity, overwhelm not just specific truths but the notion of truth generally; state-sanctioned supremacy of one class or race over others; and a commonly held sense of public helplessness so deeply felt as to result in widespread lunacy. Check, check, check, check.

March 08

I BEGIN PARING LIFE DOWN. PART of this is the coming split with Viv, and part is the clarifying impact of the fire evacuation a few months ago. I don't want to unduly clutter my mile-high Dubai penthouse with more possessions than it has room for. I make midnight trips to the canyon library where I leave bags of books at the door till finally one night there's a sign: *Stop leaving bags of books at the door.* What remains are dream books, books of secrets, the *Arabian Nights* & *Ozma of Oz* & the selected Emily Dickinson, *Journey to the End of the Night* & *Labyrinths* & *The Book of Disquiet*, *The Zoo Where You're Fed to God* & the *Adventures of Huckleberry Finn* that I last read 40 yrs ago. No writer does himself any good reading *Huckleberry Finn* too many times. It's a novel by which he can count on being humiliated. Now on the verge of a dark & mean America 3.0 that will negate the country's two preceding versions, it's well to remember that the writing of *Finn* began around the time Frederick Douglass published his autobiography, little more than a decade after the Civil War & the death of Slave America — an historical novel then, of the earlier enslaved America that a newly free republic meant to kill, the America of the Asterisk whose death throes the current America still shakes off. If *Huckleberry Finn* remains the great American novel, it's because not only its voice remains radically American but its subversions. In Huck & his flight for freedom with Jim can still be seen the aspirational America, the America in pursuit of an uncharted self lost in the dark never-healing heart whose bruise is distilled in the lexicon's single most vile word, the word that refers to Jim's color & explodes like a bomb every time it's read or said or heard. Nothing attests to the book's power like its capacity to unsettle & remind us who we are, which is both Huck & Jim on the run and also the ravenous & despicable nation that runs them down and, all this time later, runs down the rest of us....

March 09

WHEN NOTHING ASTONISHES ANYMORE, AN ASTONISHING poll reveals that more than half of Republicans believe Trump is a greater President than Lincoln. So I'm not overly ruffled by Congress' single most spectacular display of nitwittery in human form, Texan Republican Louie Gohmert, talking of civil war if Trump is removed from office. For once Gohmert gets it right. This civil war — albeit a cold one — has been going on at least a quarter century unless, of course, the last 150 yrs have been a Civil War that never ended.

Another lunch with my Mom. Try as I do to avoid politics, halfway thru the meal she says, "I don't want to get into politics, but — " at which point we get into politics. I'm reminded that the Fox "News" she watches barely acknowledges laws of the molecular universe let alone facts of the President's corruption. Soon I'm ranting at her in the restaurant which no one deserves at the age of 92. She allows that the President can be unseemly at times but insists he doesn't get credit for "accomplishments" she can't name. She lets slip — in a manner more regretful than reproachful — her conviction that going to UCLA is where I went wrong. This is her maternal way of absolving me and I admit it accounts for all the strange dreams over the decades of clandestine Marxist professors breaking into my dorm room as I slept & installing this chip at the base of my skull. Startling how badly the job was botched in typically soviet style, with some shoddy transistor picked up at Radio Shack for $7.98. Programmed to bolt upright at dawn singing the Internationale, I roll over & go back to sleep.

March 12

WAKING THIS MORNING, I'M CERTAIN MY brain pulses & my body throbs. How much of this is neurosis & how much a virus that hasn't existed before? "I just want some peace," a woman sighs in line at the grocery store, while behind me another woman in her best Palisades polish insists whatever's happening is Obama's fault. This is one of the strangest weeks

I've lived thru — market shelves wiped clean of toilet paper, in case your symbolism stash runs low. Last time I saw anything like it, I was a kid during the Cuban Missile Crisis.

March 15

THE IDES. DAYS OF THE FEVER. It's the nature of this new über-pneumonia that no one knows when it began, now that we've discovered it's been here longer than anyone realized. Almost overnight it snuck into our lives....

The President, however, brings good tidings. The new pandemic is no big deal, barely anything. Another Democratic hoax to hurt the stock market — which has been going off one cliff after another in recent days — and to hurt him. Surely you weren't so stupid as to think it's all about anything but him? When was the last time anything was about anything but him? It will go away by itself this summer like a miracle. Hey, wear the stupid mask if you want, that all the stupid doctors say to wear, but you look stupid in it and he's not wearing it b/c he doesn't look stupid anytime anywhere for anything. He's on speed-dial in terms of public appearances, setting the tone in briefings that range from begrudging to bemused to self-designation as a wartime President in an American Blitz. He reassures everyone there's nothing to blame him for. At a press conference today he says, "I don't take responsibility at all."

March 17

IT'S OFTEN BEEN INTERPRETED AS MISANTHROPIC behavior bordering on rude, but in fact I've been "self-quarantining" my whole life. Allow me to share my expertise. Don't talk to anyone. Don't see anyone. Read books & watch movies & let that constitute the entirety of your interaction with the species. Live inside your head where little imaginary friends are nearly as smart & interesting as you are. Soon you'll be pretty OK with the whole thing, 17 hrs out of 24. The hours you don't social distance are called "sleeping." Your whole life they said you were crazy, but who's laughing now! There, that's how it's done. I pronounce you graduated. Go forth, Social Distancers of 2020, ye alumni of alienation.

March 19

WHO HAS IT & WHO DOESN'T? Is this Day 12, 27, 43? The new plague doesn't follow a calendar. In lieu of widespread testing weeks or months away, with the United States currently lagging behind the likes of Greece & Czechoslovakia, better to assume we all have Covid & act accordingly? Exceptions are kids filling Florida beaches during spring break. Also supporters of the President who take their stand on ideological barricades against the amassed elite forces of smarty-pants actuality. As someone who's been trading in the cheap romance of apocalypse for years, I stutter for words no matter how hackneyed. Reality 1, My Imagination 0.

Mother Nature has pushed the pause button on civilization. Purely by chance, six months ago I devised a seminar called "Entropia" — not to be confused with dystopia or surrealism — for this upcoming spring quarter. This is the fiction & cinema of Things Coming Apart, not just societal disorder but the psychic disintegration of history, religion, culture, identity, sexuality, sanity & Meaning itself. Not just cosmic anarchy but pandemonium at its most personal. Now I try to reconfigure the seminar in a way that aligns with Pandemia's reconfigurations. Meanwhile all night I percolate viruses inwardly. One of the pandemic's inescapable byproducts in the days/weeks/months to come will be the extent to which everyone goes nuts. However great, the physical toll will be outdistanced by the psychic.

March 22

THE LESS THE PRESIDENT DOES, the more his poll numbers inch up. Maybe he deduces not unreasonably that if he stops doing anything at all, the whole country will be behind him. Moreover his approval numbers rise as his "trust" numbers decline, which is to say the less people believe him, the more they like him. We assume he's in the process of self-destructing when actually he's in the process of getting himself reelected. Yet again: Trump isn't something happening to us, rather we're happening to ourselves & Trump is its exhibition. His craziness is the index of ours.

March 25

IT AMUSES VIV TO POINT OUT that when we moved into our house, within 24 hrs my books & music & movies were all on the shelves in alphabetical order even as everything else remains in dishevelment two decades later. It would be foolish to deny this since it's entirely true & anyone who knows me knows damned well it's true. I could argue it's a matter of trying to arrange the world around me so as to better deal with the havoc in my head, and that might be partly true too, or we could just say I'm obsessive & leave it at that....

Parenthood isn't a portal to bliss. It's the more terrifying entry to something fearsome you didn't know existed when everything in your life was about you. More than 20 yrs ago Parker crawled into my office one afternoon as I sat staring into space, and before my aghast gaze pulled every meticulously sequenced book off all the lower shelves till they were bare, and then put all the books back in an order *that made no sense.* As I sat pondering his mysterious classifications trying to determine if he was another agent of chaos or the next Dalai Lama — this is a kid who, at the age of five, solemnly pronounced one afternoon at Sea World, "Dad, if X is nothing, then infinity must be One" — I said to myself, The new order is here. Fatherhood is going to demand flexibility. Flash forward 20 yrs to an infernal plague-planet where I've succumbed to current reality & decided there's nothing to do but disrupt alphabetization altogether. I've now designated three shelves apart from the others to hold the books & movies

I'll grab when flames come fretting up the highway again. I've a feeling this isn't the only manner in which our priorities now are subject to the whims of reality in revolt. The havoc isn't just in my head anymore & maybe never was. We're all agents of chaos now, assuming we're not Dalai Lamas.

April 07

IN THE GREAT LOCKDOWN OF 2020, Viv & I enter mediation. Neither of us wants to fight.

April 08

I'VE TRADED IN THE DUBAI PENTHOUSE of my future for a bunker at world's end. Excuse the mess. Since this is inside my head, the interior decorating leaves something to be desired. The industrial-size refrigerator is packed with filets, Chopin vodka, a dozen cartons of Ben & Jerry's Chocolate Therapy. The medicine cabinet is stocked with antacids & lexapro while I cross fingers that my migraines don't outrace the supply of sumatriptan. The bookshelves are lined with what volumes I had time to grab as the apocalypse licked my heels. On my laptop are Eno, Dusty Springfield, Duke Ellington & my *Sinatra at 3 a.m.* playlist for enjoying my steak & martini to the howl of nuclear winds crossing the Santa Monica plains above.

At the end of the bunker which, being inside my head, is as large or small as I think it is at any given moment, in the shadows of the future's unmarked doorway — that door that swings both in & out, keeping me out & luring me in — looms the anointed Executioner of Memory. He looks like whatever you think he looks like. May bear a resemblance to me or you. Wields whatever devastating device you think…a blade, rope, pistol, garotte, a live wire sparking between his fingers. Beyond that door he waits to kill my memories rather than my body or brain or heart — so he's not necessarily an exterminator but a liberator. He may be my deliverer, freeing me of remembrances that stutter on repeat….

The memories aren't forgotten. Rather they're just corpses strewn over whatever landscape is past that door. I don't yet have the courage for this execution maybe b/c after I go thru this door there's only one door left. I indulge these absurd fantasies that aren't altogether acceptable let alone admirable. If it's not a bunker at the end of the world or a Dubai residency in one of those structures that twist to the clouds, I plot a nonstop flying suite on Emirates that takes me from one international lounge to another — high above the entropic world — in moonlit baudelairean derangement.

April 19

MY GUESS IS I'M NOT THE only one who wakes every morning to a renewed sense of enormity that has to be re-absorbed on a daily basis. My guess is I'm not the only one for whom, with every morning, the sense becomes stronger we're living thru a time so strange & irrevocable there's no going back. Watch an hour of news or read an hour of press and there's no getting around a sense of national teetering — on the edge economically, politically, socially, geographically....

Let's not pretend anything has brought us to this point but capitalism gone berserk, religiosity contemptuous of humanism, governance hostile to truth. As peaceful & constructive a revolution as possible is called for but a revolution in any case of any sort, a revolution of focus, determination & dare we say ruthlessness. Tho I haven't kept up with everything he's done in recent years, by way of focus, determination & ruthlessness Bob Dylan was one of the revelations of my early life along with Ray Charles, changing everything I thought about not just music but art, writing, creativity & myself insofar as I thought about myself in those terms at all. From the most dispassionate standpoint Dylan's new song, "Murder Most Foul," is uneven — my heart sinks a bit at the opening lines — but builds to something over 18 mins that renders quibbles irrelevant. The song isn't, as would seem, about John Kennedy's assassination. It returns to the assassination as allegory, and tho that allegory is as familiar as specious contemplations of "lost American innocence," this elegy could only have been managed by someone no less deserving than 116 other recipients of a Nobel Prize that never went to Kafka, Joyce, Tolstoy, Ibsen, Woolf, Proust, Rilke, Cather, Borges, Pynchon, Lispector, Ocampo, Bowles, DeLillo, Henry Miller or Philip Dick. Marking a moment when America is a precarious proposition, the song speaks to an ambition unmatched in post-19th Century American music by anyone except Ellington & Miles Davis....

April 25

THE PRESIDENT FAMOUSLY BRAGGED HE COULD shoot someone on Fifth Avenue & people would still vote for him. Now he boasts he can shoot *you* on Fifth Avenue and, whoever you are, you'll still drag your own bleeding bullet-ridden body to the polling place on his behalf. Got a note a couple days ago from someone I don't know named Dean who went to a convention of the National Association of Music Merchants in Anaheim. To Dean's thinking, this proves the pandemic is a fraud b/c otherwise everyone there would have gotten sick. I appreciate that Dean apparently is a merchandiser who can ill afford a slowdown of the recovery that was created by the President's predecessor, and a conversation about balancing the national economic health with the citizenry's medical health might be valuable but for Dean's references to "hysterical libtards" along with rhetoric that's equal parts invective, horse-shit & pre-adolescent sarcasm. In the name of what cause does the Right keep humiliating itself with claims silly on their face and dangerous to themselves & other people who mean something to them, assuming there are other people who mean something to them?

I'm embarrassed to say I was 19 before I wondered what "philosophy" was worth lying to myself. Half a century ago when I began outgrowing the politics in which I was raised, I noticed part of my problem wasn't with ideology, tho as proved by the civil rights movement more than anything, conservatism was constructed on ethical notions increasingly problematic.

More inescapably it became apparent that many of the most fervent conservatives were…I want to be precise in my terminology here…assholes, and that I was on my way to becoming an asshole too. There's something hateful in the wiring of an Attorney General who derides "social distancing" as "hiding under [our] beds" because he's incapable of considering the possibility that people aren't just protecting their own selves but their families & loved ones & neighbors and, yes — most anathema to the right-wing sensibility — perfect strangers who are part of a community. Any self-respecting right-winger's words to live by are: Fuck community. Any community that isn't a marketplace just cuts into the profit share. Two of the most revered words in the progressive lexicon — "social contract" — are distrusted by right-wingers b/c they're about nothing less than what it means to be a country, and for Americans that answer is anywhere between anarchy & collectivism. The Right concludes it's reasonable making people choose between living & voting, it's reasonable making people die to vote, because "fuck community" is code for fuck democracy.

When I was 12 my Mom took me to Downtown L.A. to hear Barry Goldwater. This anticipated more than either of us knew our conflicted political relationship to come, since positions that Goldwater held then & years afterward wound up well to his party's left. The problem for my Mom & me now — as I think is true these days for other American moms & sons — is we don't even agree anymore on the east/west/north/south of a common compass. Not since acceptance of the earth being round & circling the sun has the science on anything been as universal as on climate change, but as weather becomes more freakish, by the lights of Fox "News" this only disproves global warming because, you know, sometimes it's really cold outside. One Oklahoma Senator brought a snowball to the Senate floor as refutation.

About 10 yrs ago during the Obamacare debate, Mom called to say, "Boy, your socialist President really has screwed things up," alarmed that my family's health coverage might be dropped and, in the looming Red Terror, she would lose her Medicare. It seemed beside the point to remind her that half a century before, she decried the Medicare she now cherishes as "socialized medicine." For the Right, "socialism" has been such an effective shtick for so long as to render irrelevant the cerebral limits of Fox commentary ("Socialism sucks!") let alone objective standards by which Obamacare is to the right of the health-care plan proposed by Roger Ailes's old boss Richard Nixon, before it was stupidly killed by Ted Kennedy for not being radical enough. Socialism has come to mean any government involvement in the economy whatsoever, which is to say we've been a socialist country since Alexander Hamilton created a national bank in the 1790s, none of which matters to the Right any more than facts regarding the weather. That there are two Americas now is obvious with the only question being, What's this civil war about? Each side fights for something different. One America fights to be better. The other fights to be richer.

An outspoken liberal in her youth, my Mom was the more ideological of my parents, both of whom grew up New Deal Democrats. By 11 days she missed being old enough to vote for Truman in 1948. My Dad also voted for Truman, but tho he remained a registered Democrat, he never voted Democratic again. After that began the rightward political trajectory of so many New Deal kids, which accelerated in response to the tumult of the '60s, accompanied by middle-class ascension & alarm that Soviet communism was winning the Cold War. My own fascination with politics derived from an interest in the drama of American history. By the time I was 12, I was writing stories about Lincoln & Nathan Hale, revealing a suspiciously romantic enthusiasm for patriots making the ultimate sacrifice. My inner cornball holding sway, I could recite the Gettysburg Address & name all the presidents in order. Enthralled by Jefferson's maxim that "government is best which governs least" (there's now some question whether he said this), I believed the Bill of Rights is the greatest political document ever written & still believe it, even if it was less an addendum to the Constitution than a rebuttal by the Constitution's greatest skeptic, its so-called father James Madison. Since the liberalism of the '60s was as smug as the conservatism of the future would be sanctimonious, I was pleased when a high school teacher called me "dangerous." What teenager doesn't want to be dangerous when he's so undangerous in so many other ways?

The conservatism I embraced was the proverbial whole greater than the sum of the parts, its libertarian emphasis on individual freedom overriding stuff I considered incidental.

To the extent I understood it, a liberal idea that arose from the Great Crash of '29 — that there should be a division between commercial & investment banks, without which the great crash of 2008 became possible — sounded sensible, maybe even conservative, and I didn't really know what the Tennessee Valley Authority was or what it meant that Goldwater mused openly about selling it. Goldwater mused openly about a lot of strange shit. Verging on my teens, I finally became troubled in the summer of '64 when Goldwater was nominated at the Republican Convention in San Francisco. Liberals recoiled when he said "extremism in the pursuit of liberty is no vice," but Tom Paine & Patrick Henry not to mention Jefferson said the same thing, more or less. But if I wasn't savvy enough to comprehend Goldwater's provocation, the mob fury gripping the convention in TV's crude black & white was harder to ignore. More instinctually than I could articulate, I had the feeling these were people I wouldn't want to be in the same room with. Still too young to fathom what was meant by the better angels of our nature, nevertheless I experienced my first sense of political alienation, and it was from those whom I thought were on my side. My growing realization that conservatives were on the wrong side of the times' great crucible, racial justice, rendered me not so much a leftist as a nomad, esp given ideology's reflexive commitment to predetermined conclusions. Clumsily I sorted my way thru the intellectual dishonesties of conservatives who take a strict-constructionist view of the Bill of Rights except for the 2nd Amendment, which they interpret broadly enough to arm

14-yr-olds with automatic weapons, and liberals who take a broad view of the Bill of Rights except for the 2nd Amendment, where they become strict constructionists clinging to fine print about militias. Beyond the north stars of life, liberty, justice & pursuit of chilled martinis at Musso & Frank, over the years I've become a situationist, and you don't have to be an ideologue of any stripe to know that a nation facing a crisis like a pandemic must respond nationally or what's the point of being a nation?

I blame no one who finds my political evolution immaterial. We live in a novel moment for which nothing provides a precedent, when no one can accept any fate as inevitable & still retain his sanity. A pandemic no one can see or measure coincides with political blight on a scale previously untold. The ultimate emblem of American self-betrayal, the Confederate flag — for which even halfhearted rationalizations are akin to justifying the swastika as a sanskrit symbol — is on more prominent display than in half a century. Add to this a simple truth about the American character which is that we don't do ambiguity. We like our destinies clear-cut. We like our turning points chartable from years out, 1944 D-Days already in sight by summers of '42. A long black tunnel with no discernible dot of light at the end isn't the American shadowbahn of choice. For all its protestations of faith, the country's bottomless secret is that faith has had an expiration date since 1945's articulation of self-oblivion's deepest nuclear desire. Now, in as exquisite a tick of the American clock as any of us has heard, we're on the verge of a chaos unidentified, unsurpassed, unbound....

May – July 2020

We meet ourselves time and again in a thousand disguises on the path of life.

Jung

May 06

On the 70-inch flatscreen TV in my flying suite, somewhere on the other side of civilization's demise — as documented by my ongoing film festival of *Weekend*, *Demonlover*, *Melancholia*, *Lost Highway*, *The Passenger*, *Eros + Massacre...* — Tarkovsky's "stalker" in the movie of the same name longs to be a holy fool if only he can find the faith for it. When he can't, he's an "eternal prisoner," a man of eyes & ears leading two other guys of words & numbers out of their ruins into a forbidden Zone of which the hub is the Room, a kind of decrepit cathedral to where the faithless make pilgrimage....

May 10

What does it mean that I find it easier to tell Viv's side of the story? I'm barely comprehensible to myself. Confined to my brain since I was four by a speech disorder that I share with the Democratic nominee for President, I've made myself comfortable here. I have to remind myself that nobody else hears the voice in my head that confirms with every passing word how — there's no getting around it — I certainly am the most fascinating person I know.

Viv wants to tell the kids about our split sooner rather than later. She needs the clarity. I so dread it sometimes I can barely function. I can't decide if Parker will take it harder or

Zema, who's known disruption since spending her first two years handed off by her mother to her grandmother to an orphanage in Addis Ababa to a new American family. I'm back to worrying about money....

May 14

BARACK OBAMA HAS BEEN CIRCUMSPECT to a fault these past three years, but this morning he finally says something critical of the President's handling (sic) of the pandemic. On air the Majority Leader admonishes the black man to mind his place. It's possible that, as Deep Throat advised Bob Woodward in 1973, Republicans just aren't that bright. Of all the Democrats they can be campaigning against, they're apparently dying to run against the guy who polls 25 points more popular than Trump, 40 points more popular than the Senate's leading Republican, and who a plurality of Americans consider the best President of their lifetimes. "Why don't *you* have a drink with McConnell?" Obama once joked, and Mitch still hasn't gotten over it.

May 18

CONFLICTING INFORMATION THIS MORNING ABOUT THE pandemic, or should I say conflicting information about the "information"? Armed militants storm statehouses over being asked to wear masks. A leading specialist fired by the President testifies before the House that the country faces the "darkest winter in modern history" due to weeks squandered by an administration that lies about everything.

Thinking about it the past couple weeks, I realize that beneath *Stalker*'s reverence is dread that the Zone won't deliver us from doubt after all. "When a man thinks of the past, he becomes kinder," the stalker half declares, half wonders. But what happens when thinking of the future makes us meaner? That Tarkovsky, increasingly at odds with the godless Soviet Union, is the most spiritually obsessed of great filmmakers isn't ironic but inevitable. He's determined to map his inner quest, apropos for a filmmaker who would shoot a movie like *Stalker* all over again when the original negative proved unusable. *Stalker* is outside chronology — three hours that feel as consuming as lifetimes & fleeting as moments. When a dream is a memory of the future, the future is authenticated not by what's answered but what isn't. The stalker's life is haunted by its questions.

May 23

IN COLLEGE, MY LIFE WAS HAUNTED by its questions. I had doubts about everything & doubts about the doubts. I found silly the revolutionary sentiments in pop music I otherwise loved. I wouldn't put a poster of Mao on my wall any more than I'd have one of Hitler. Left-wing ideologues I knew reminded me of right-wing ideologues I knew, including the one I had known best: me. The extent to which ideology hijacks independent thought was all the more confirmed by how long it took me to see it. Ideology is a psychological construct posing as a theoretical one. This is how fervent communist totalitarians of the '30s turned into fervent anti-communist totalitarians of the '50s....

The Republican Party's existence has been marked by five incarnations in its century & a half, peaking early with Lincoln, its first President & the country's greatest. The second Republican age culminated at the outset of the last century with Theodore Roosevelt, the third with Eisenhower and the fourth with Reagan, whose harbingers were Goldwater & Richard Nixon and whose coda was the Bushes. Turning out to be the conservative Jesus for whom Goldwater proved only John the Baptist, Reagan personified a conservatism that crossed eloquence on behalf of liberty with a trust in the power of a right-wing state, whatever he said otherwise.

While Reagan's election as President in 1980 appeared to be the apotheosis of what Goldwater started, in fact conservatism & Reagan each remade themselves in the image of the other. Under Reagan the size of the federal government exploded. The war on drugs grew more ruthless. Antagonism to the freedom of women grew more vehement. Cynicism about science, particularly as it had to do with the environment, grew more pronounced. The Justice Department paid unsettling attention to what adults read & watched. New impulses distinguished the new Right, whose enmity to centralized state power was matched by an adoration of centralized corporate power — an overt abandonment of the principles of decentralization & a free market. Liberty as conservatism's core priority was displaced by a new priority, "values," by which the Right invariably meant sexual behavior, by which it invariably meant women & homosexuals. Particularly profound was a reconceptualization of the Republic as one where citizens are bound not by a secular Constitution but an unwritten Christian covenant subjecting free will to a theocratic ethos. What once identified itself as a freedom movement became a wealth/religion/authority movement. The new conservatism now spoke of the Bill of Rights with veiled contempt. Paying lip service to freedom in the abstract, the only two freedoms that conservatives defended were the right to make a profit & the right to own a gun.

The fifth Republican incarnation that ultimately yielded Trump was that of Newton Leroy Gingrich of Georgia in the mid-'90s. Not even Trump better represents the party over the past 30 yrs. Gingrich was the embodiment of a conservative "intellectualism" that fashioned itself Churchillian. In the wake of liberalism's retreat at the end of the last century, this conservatism aspired to bring to Reaganism the one thing it lacked — unforgiving rigor in place of what Gingrich perceived as the Old Man's misplaced congeniality. Gingrich's view of America was nihilist in a way that would be matched a decade later only by Mitch McConnell & a decade after that by House members like Jim Jordan, Devin Nunes & Matt Gaetz. The bloodlust Gingrich elicited so routinely from debate audiences in his campaign for the 2012 Republican nomination anticipated the Trump rallies of four years later. The Gingrich model wasn't simply an edgier conservatism. More thrillingly to the rank & file it was ruthlessness matched by rhetoric that mixed the incendiary tone of the '60s with the faux erudition of adjectives & adverbs at odds with each other ("I'm mildly astonished..."). Gingrich's modus operandi has always been to attach mockery to cerebral-sounding absurdities about Kenyan colonialism that, in a tradition begun by Lenin & refined by Goebbels, isn't merely dishonest but brazenly so. Crack open the Gingrich soul and locusts emerge, a pestilence merciless & biblical in scope, while better angels rush to its void in a shriek of self-extermination. Because Gingrich is a phony (Goldwater hated him), it's almost fitting that his career was crushed by Trump's more Barnum & Bailey version of an unscrupulousness unhindered by shame over, say, abandoned wives. Gingrich left his first when she was critically ill. "She's not young or pretty enough to be the wife of a President," he said at the time, "and besides, she has cancer."

May 25

AFTER COLLEGE I SPENT A DECADE on & off in Europe. From a distance I thought about America amid an overload of the sensory & historic. I was rousted by soldiers in Madrid when Franco was dying & I was in San Sebastián as tanks in the streets put down a Basque uprising. The day after I read *To the Lighthouse* in Hyde Park, the IRA bombed it, and I heard the Clash play in Brixton where Prime Minister Maggie Thatcher scolded broke jobless Brits for not being made of sterner stuff.

When Reagan became President, I watched Parisians march in their boulevards convinced there was going to be nuclear war. A generation later, my own kids have their own political identities, even as they find little allure in memorizing presidents — Parker has a libertarian streak that runs parallel to his socialist streak, and when Zema was seven she was overheard by neighbors railing at her playmates, "Don't even get me started on Paul Ryan!" Now she reads Du Bois, Angela Davis, books with titles like *Making of the Black Radical Tradition*.

A video surfaces tonight from Minneapolis of an African American man arrested by a handful of police officers for allegedly passing a counterfeit $20 bill. Lying handcuffed on the street, he struggles for air while one of the officers kneels on his neck as passing pedestrians beg the officer to let the man breathe. It's not clear when exactly the suspect is dead.

May 27

EVERY TIME THE INITIAL RESPONSE IS reactive by those of us who are white, it's an attempt to make black reality about ourselves. "Well, my relatives came from Ireland, and the Irish were discriminated against too, so...." No. Black American reality is singular in its circumstances. Kidnapped from their homeland across terrible oceans that few survived, dehumanized to the status of property, segregated & lynched with ecstatic savagery — all this is the bloody asterisk that nothing can really make right. Patriots who love their country are bound to try anyway. Those of us white may never fully deserve the forgiveness of those not, but this blood-soaked real estate won't be worthy till forgiveness is at least asked.

Tonight mid-pandemic Minneapolis is on fire. There's a sense of American collapse at every level — atonement is at hand. 2020 might remind me more of 1968 if it wasn't worse. In 1968 American society came apart, in 2020 the American Idea comes apart. When that woman stood up at a town hall & shouted, "If we have to have a dictator, I hope it's Trump," that was new. Nobody said that in the '60s tho some surely thought it. Pandemic, economic ruin, police killing African Americans...even voters who have no fixed impression of Trump, whoever such voters can be, have the indelible impression that the President embodies it all. Whatever else voters feel about him, they're increasingly exhausted. The election is being decided now in homes of the broken & isolated, hospitals of the sick & dying, streets of fire & fury.

June 01

IT'S NOT GOING TO MAKE ANYONE forget John Lewis but today I assume a lonely vigil along Highway 27 in the Twin Peaks of L.A. called Topanga Canyon. One side of the sign Viv made says BLM (Black Lives Matter) and the other says VOTE HIM OUT. Fifteen thousand cars pass thru the canyon each day between the Valley & Pacific Coast Highway. Lots of support from passersby including beeps, waves & thumbs up, tho it's always possible they're raising a different digit.

June 02

TEN EXTRAORDINARY DAYS IN THE COUNTRY'S life. A national demonstration unlike any since the '60s hasn't just coalesced but grown greater each day, made up of a greater swath of American life than ever before. Thousands of people in hundreds of American towns all march in the midst of the greatest pandemic in a century, the greatest economic collapse in 90 yrs & a presidency more openly hostile to democracy than any known in modern times. Lots of resistance on the Left to the tainted anti-trumpism of disaffected Republicans, but me, I take my Sauls-turned-Pauls on any Damascan road I can find them. Yes they're all complicit — what an insight! But is it so hard understanding that the most immediate task is saving what's left of democracy? Last night the President gassed a peaceful crowd outside the White House so he could walk to the local church & hold up a Bible whose only value to him is as a public relations tool.

Tomorrow I take my Mom to a doctor's appointment. The 10-min drive won't be half over before I hear from her how Democrats want to abolish police. I'll explain at some length that's not what the new chant "Defund the police" means, that what it really means is "reform the police" or "reimagine policing from the ground up," and for once she's going to ask a damn good question — if that's what it means, why don't we say that? "Defunding" the police is going to be the talking point as long as the Trump Right can make it so, b/c otherwise they have nothing to say and so wasn't it nice of us to give them something? I'm sure if we tried harder we could sabotage ourselves further, just when the public is on the right side of the issue while Democrats open a lead in polls. Fifty years ago anti-Vietnam protesters — on the right side of history & increasingly on the right side of public opinion — gave away the game when some stupid kid burned an American flag on TV.

The hand in the pocket. It's midnight & I'm tired but my brain keeps going round & round as to why now, as to what it is about the George Floyd video that's different after all the other videos of police barbarity, and it's the hand in the pocket. Not just the act of murder but the gesture of contempt, of hubris, of an officer who's done something like this, if not as lethally, 100 times before. A cop for whom this is as routine as Starbucks in the morning. His hand in his pocket as he kneels on Floyd's neck unperturbed by passersby asking him to please stop — this is what finally became too much. Of course it should have been too much long ago. It should have been too much centuries ago. It should never have taken this long. But this time it's not just the act but the manifest attitude, like a hunter casually crouched on a still thrashing animal he's just shot in the woods, with Floyd's pleas for breath no more than the strangled sounds the animal makes at the end. Whether some significant change comes of all that's happened, there will be consequences either way. This will be one of our indelible images, one of our important pieces of tragic footage for however much longer our history lasts, like the Zapruder film or the towers falling.

June 14

TODAY I TAKE ZEMA & A friend to a Black Lives Matter protest march in Hollywood. It's a good Sunday for a march, warm but breezy. The crowd is large enough that, in the middle of it, there's no sense of where the beginning is or the end. Along the march bystanders cheer from the sidewalks & the windows of apartments. The marchers are sprawling & diverse, people of all races & orientations wearing masks. We pass the Comedy Club on Sunset & cut down Crescent Heights to Santa Monica Blvd where everyone turns west, a guy with a bullhorn leading chants. Everyone seems to have backed off "Defund the police."

June 20

TULSA, SITE OF THE PRESIDENT'S DESPERATE return to the MAGA rallies that so sustain him...except tonight, engulfed by Black Lives Matter & the pandemic, the Bank of Oklahoma Center where the rally is held is two-thirds empty. The *Washington Post* reports that in the hours before the President's rally, campaign workers were directed to go thru the center & remove thousands of social-distancing stickers from the seats, putting the President's most loyal supporters at risk. "If the war is lost," Hitler snarled to those around him in his last months, "then it's of no concern to me whether the German people perish. I wouldn't shed a single tear for them, because they don't deserve better."

July 05

TWO WEEKS SINCE MY LAST ENTRY. Tonight Viv & I tell the kids we're splitting. Parker takes the news surprisingly well — he may have sensed something or heard talk thru the walls. Zema feels it harder & shuts herself in her room. Abandoned by her birth mother, abandoned by the family of the birth father who wouldn't acknowledge she was his, now she may feel abandoned in some way deeper than whether we're all still living in the same house, as we'll continue to do for the pandemic's course. All the while she navigates the shit that comes with being 15 & the only black member of a white family in a racist society. Oh, I guess we're capitalizing now, so…the only Black member. I don't get the new punctuation-correctness but that goes with being an old white guy, or is it "old White guy"?

Reports today that Trump pressures South Dakota's governor to carve his face into Rushmore's mountainside along with Washington, Jefferson, Lincoln & Roosevelt.

July 07

OVER THE PAST FEW DAYS ON Fox "News", manchild Tucker Carlson — adopted into the Swanson frozen food empire & having spent half his life emulating the bow ties of conservative éminence grise George Will — attacks Tammy Duckworth, the U.S. Senator from Illinois, as a "moron," "coward" & "deeply silly" person who "hates America." This past weekend Senator Duckworth questioned whether we should leave up statues of George Washington who owned slaves. I disagree with her position but she left half her body on an Iraqi battlefield defending my right to do that. She left half her body on an Iraqi battlefield defending Carlson's right to call her a moron & coward. This morning she answers, "Does Tucker Carlson want to walk a mile in my legs," which are titanium, "and tell me whether I love America?"

July 10

EVERY DAY BETWEEN NOW & THE election, Biden and the Democrats should be asking: Mr. President, at what number of deaths among supporters at your rallies is your reelection no longer worth it? Mr. President, you knew in January that a pandemic was coming — how high does the death toll have to reach before you stop telling us it's over? Mr. President, is the reason you're willing to risk American children to the virus because you can't put them in cages on the border with those who have been there two years? Mr. President, was your two-hour meeting with Vladimir Putin in Helsinki when you destroyed the notes the same one where you told him it was OK to put a bounty on the heads of American soldiers? Mr. President, the Supreme Court has ruled you're going to have to show your tax returns sooner or later — why not now? Mr. President, what did your predecessor Mr. Lincoln misunderstand about the Civil War that leads you to support the defeated Confederacy? Mr. President, what did Frederick Douglass misunderstand about racism that leads you to support white supremacists?

It's revealed that Tucker Carlson's chief writer on Fox has been posting online, under a pseudonym, racist comments that bear a striking similarity to those made by Carlson on air.

July 17

TODAY IT'S ANNOUNCED THAT SUPREME COURT Justice Ruth Bader Ginsburg has relapsed with pancreatic cancer. Viv's father was taken by this particularly vicious disease. "Democrats," reports the *Washington Post*, "fear that if [Ginsburg] died or had to resign, Mr. Trump and his Republican allies in the Senate, led by Mitch McConnell of Kentucky, the majority leader, would quickly try to install a conservative successor even as the November election is imminent." Keep a prayer.

Then in the waning minutes before midnight comes news John Lewis is dead. Like the rest of the country, I watched a few weeks ago when Lewis stood on one of the huge yellow letters BLACK LIVES MATTER now inscribing the boulevard leading to the White House, supposedly readable from outer space. The country's embodiment of whatever moral authority America still has, Lewis must have been in tremendous pain standing in that street. I wonder if the country is worthy of his obituary.

July 18

IN THE SUMMER OF '64, AS I watched the televised Republican Convention, Lewis already was working on the 1965 Voting

Rights Act. Its precursor the Civil Rights Act was being passed by the Senate on the momentum of John Kennedy's martyrdom. If not as practically significant as voting rights, symbolically the Civil Rights Act was as momentous a piece of legislation as any since the 13th Amendment ending slavery a century before. Twenty-nine senators voted against the law: Goldwater was one of them. Following World War II he desegregated the Arizona National Guard, was a proponent of integrating the nation's military forces, and in the Senate supported every previous civil-rights bill including the '64 bill in an earlier, less expansive form. But tho I accept at face value the constitutional rationale Goldwater gave for his vote, which was that the government shouldn't have the power to dictate the conduct of a private business, even in the day I had an uneasy sense of some bigger picture being missed. Whatever were Goldwater's reasons, there's no doubt much of Goldwater's subsequent presidential support was racist & most of the anger I watched at the convention that nominated him was white wrath. Not putting too fine a point on it, as much as any single person it was my first political hero — along with any cognizant person who supported him, including overzealous white boys from the San Fernando Valley — who planted the seed of trumpism. *Je m'accuse.*

Politics is personal, which is the point of this journal if it has one. I'm aware how self-serving this is. This white boy had half a century to cover his tracks, and it's disingenuous to suggest the changes I went thru were born of wisdom. A cultural explosion rocked the decade around me. The facts of the civil rights movement became more inexorable than worries about Cold War totalitarianism. With Black people being hosed down on TV and beset by vicious dogs & vicious sticks swung by vicious cops, rhetoric about states' rights sounded hollow. If Jeffersonian individualism remained an ideal, history provided indisputable examples in the 1860s & 1960s how sometimes only national resolution will secure individual freedom in the face of local oppression. Suffice it to say that when I glance back at myself over my shoulder, I don't much like what I see — someone rigid & disapproving with politics to match. Nonetheless, even for me the rightness of racial justice became a bright line readable from outer space.

July 19

TONIGHT IN PORTLAND, OREGON, MEN WEARING unmarked uniforms arrive in black unmarked cars to spirit away protesting citizens. The social contract frays, a racial reckoning is at hand, proto-totalitarianism takes its toll on truth, a plague batters a nation with neither the strategy nor will for battling back, and the only thing to be assumed with semi-certainty is that, six months from tomorrow, a President is scheduled to take the oath of office. No more time for squabbles or sniping, snits or bullshit. Get ready.

Viv & I have dinner together with both kids for the first time since announcing our separation. We talk about the black cars in Portland. Parker remains dubious of Biden's chances. There's growing chatter on the news about who Biden will pick as his vice-president — the media focuses on former National Security Adviser Susan Rice. Viv & Parker lean to Warren. I think it's going to be Duckworth or Kamala Harris. Zema disapproves of Harris's record as a former prosecutor. In less momentous news Viv mentions a 22-yr-old female teacher in Kentucky just sentenced to two years in jail & a lifetime registration as a sex offender for sending four topless photos to a 15-yr-old student. We all agree the sentence is nuts. Esp in a woke world this was poor judgment on the woman's part to say the least & she shouldn't teach again. But as a former 15-yr-old, particularly in this day & age I think the boy will overcome whatever trauma was incurred by four topless photos before this stupid young woman, barely an adult herself, survives a sentence intended to fuck up the rest of her life & trivialize sexual assault in the process.

July 20

I POST THE ABOVE. IT'S SOCIAL media, so I figure on some dissent. About an hour later I realize the post is more flippant than I intend — a lame & tone-deaf joke that the boy is more likely to feel he died & went to heaven than that he's molested — and revise it. Some respondents agree with the post. Some don't, including friends who believe I've underestimated the breach of pedagogic trust on the teacher's part & the destructive impact on the boy. By now I'm used to people teasing out from the fabric of what I write whatever thread bothers them & responding to that. I keep trying to restore the fabric.

July 21

TWENTY-FOUR HOURS AFTER THE POST, he barely knows what's hit him. It's one thing for people to tell him he's wrong. Maybe he *is* wrong. But the vitriol — particularly from members of a local "literary" community — is overwhelming. "Fucking trash." "Piece of shit." "Pro-sex with children." "Apologist for pedophilia." "Sexualizing high school teachers." "Your hard drive should be seized by the FBI." "You should be registered as a sex offender yourself."

He takes down his post but it doesn't stop. Writers who have solicited his support in the past for various ventures and former students he helped publish add their scorn. "Don't even get me started on that guy," writes one. Matters take an ominous turn when, on another site where it's assumed he wouldn't see it, a teacher he's never met identifies him as someone who makes women at his university uncomfortable. She implies something predatory. Another male teacher writes to him, "I don't want to make you paranoid, dude, but a great sum of people are talking about you because it's obvious you're the bad guy here." How fortunate to have associates who point out what a bad guy he is without wanting to make him paranoid! No one challenges his original contention that the Kentucky woman's sentence is disproportionate and unjust. Within hours they're coming for his job, which is to say his kids. Definitely third-person stuff.

July 23

DAYS AFTER HE'S TAKEN DOWN THE post and stopped responding, the attacks grow. He has a few brave champions. Another female faculty member writes privately to reassure him, while a Hollywood latina he calls Brontë — they bonded over *Wuthering Heights* — posts an articulate defense of his character.

July 26

THIS AFTERNOON HE'S VISITING HIS MOTHER when he learns a magazine interview scheduled months ago is canceled. The woman canceling the interview explains in the nicest way possible that it's been brought to her attention he's a horrible person. "Of course you have the right to free speech," she writes, "but in this case the consequence is that many women, especially educators, feel you revealed your true feelings about their worth. To speak boldly, I wonder if even now you're most concerned with being right." Her email glints like steel. How many people believe he revealed his true feelings about women's worth? How many believe he threatens women? How many believe he condones molestation? He tries to pinpoint what it is he feels most acutely. Is it anger he doesn't deserve this? Is it horror that he does? Is it frustration no one can help him? Is it shock no one will? Does he refuse to recognize a void in himself? He tries to break it down like a math problem. Receiving numerous admonitions to retain the services of an attorney, finally he does just so as not to feel helpless; he doesn't do helpless well. He does cold panic, freak-out, barely contained hysteria, indiscriminate melodrama, self-evisceration — he's accomplished at that one. But he's never mastered helpless going back to before he can remember, before life afforded him opportunities in the forms of psychodramatic romance, paralyzing compulsions, the skepticism of editorial exemplars, podcasting paragons, doyennes of decency, connoisseurs of calculation, aficionados of social aberration and now a Red Guard of literati administering justice for saying what he's still not quite sure he said. He feels allies pull away. He's too old to have been this naïve, he fumes at himself.

July 28

WNYC RUNS A PIECE ON "cancel culture." It's a term he's been avoiding because it's become ideologically loaded, the last refuge of right-wingers who have used up "snowflake," "political correctness" and "libtard." The piece features a trans woman who's been "canceled" by various venues because she said some things on social media bluntly or artlessly. The piece acknowledges cancel culture has performed a service by exposing and pressing the case against R. Kelly, Bill Cosby, Harvey Weinstein, Jeffrey Epstein. As stipulated on the program, characteristics of cancel culture include the lack of distinction between criticism and character assassination, the lack of distinction between good faith and bad, the quandary of the accused between self-defense and silence, and the way the accused becomes — as the trans woman puts it — an "evil parody" of himself in his own mind.

July 30

MORE THAN A WEEK AFTER THE original post, he wakes one morning and goes meta on everything he's written here. Is it self-justification which is to say self-martyrdom which is to say self-pity? Aren't half of you reading this right now nodding your heads, "Yup, you're an asshole all right. A great sum of people who have read anything you've written in the last forty years know you're a sex maniac. Other than sleazeballs and degenerates and misogynists, don't you realize you're the only guy who thinks like this? Otherwise all the other guys would say so, right? In this very journal you've got God Herself as a dominatrix — what's that about, *dude*? Isn't it obvious you're the bad guy here?" Then again, aren't the other half of you reading this shaking your heads, "Are you out of your freaking mind? Are you actually dredging all this up again?" Does he really believe the context of this journal changes anything? ("To speak boldly, I wonder if even now you're most concerned with being right.") Whether a writer's instincts tell him it's the only way the journal can be honest, isn't it more grandstanding?

July 31

HE CONTINUES THROUGH WHATEVER PASSAGE THIS is, be it redemption or rehabilitation or self-delusion. Stage one is climbing out the rabbit hole where everything he says winds up worse the deeper he plunges. Stage two is noting the "friends" who felt compelled to disagree with his opinion openly & harshly but felt no similar compulsion to defend his character. Stage three (where he is now) is an anger prowling for its rightful prey when he can't exclude the possibility that prey is himself. He doesn't know how many stages there are but assumes the last is grace, so far from him now that he might die before he gets there....

The President withdraws American troops from NATO. Citing the same pandemic that he claims is a hoax, he calls for delaying the presidential election for the first time in history.

August – October 2020

A people that elect corrupt politicians, imposters, thieves and traitors are not victims but accomplices.
George Orwell

August 15

THIS MORNING HE WAKES SO DAMNED tired of being afraid. He's tired of the knot in his gut that's there when he goes to bed at night and still there in the morning. He's tired of being afraid of his family vicissitudes, afraid for his kids and his Mom — he's tired of being afraid of getting old even as he's already old. He's tired of being afraid of the bad faith of "friends" who aren't that friendly and of enemies he didn't know he had. He's tired of being afraid for a pandemic nation where protesters against masks carry signs that read SELFISH AND PROUD. He's afraid that the American Reich of the moment where Baader-Meinhof patrols the culture isn't aberrational but the true one, and that it's been the true one awhile. He's tired of being afraid of tomorrow and of tomorrow's tomorrow. Does everyone feel this much a coward these days? More and more he blurts his fear in the static of his stutter, he keeps trying to will the fear away. He's tired of trying to will his way thru the fear and then when he gets to the other side, it's still there. He's afraid of his failure, of everything he's done coming to nothing. Well, actually he's gotten used to that fear, he used to be more afraid of that before his own oblivion got wrapped up with everyone else's. He's gotten used to having made no difference and to his disappearance from whatever small place in the mass consciousness he hoped to occupy. These days all he can do is flee to his writing which is the only place he's never been afraid even when he should have been. The precipice of everything is right at everyone's feet like never before. There's no getting over the fear, there's only living with it like you live with a virus that the body accommodates but never defeats. He's tired of being so afraid that he can't choose between the first person and third, so he keeps vacillating, selecting the third for however long it protects me.

August 16

CONSTANTLY REMINDED AS HE IS OF the ways he's disappointing, his inadequacy as friend, father and husband becomes the prevailing theme of his communication, or his non-communication as others would have it. Has this become more so during this terrible year or is he just more aware of it? When I go — he wakes in the night wondering to himself — will everyone say I was never quite here to begin with?

August 17

I'VE GONE INTO EXILE. I'LL STAY here awhile. I wake to thoughts that memory shuts out moments later. I find myself in half-sleep trying to remember a name, face, fact I've known forever. Can there be a worse death than losing your self before your life? I prefer the wreckage of physicality to the deterioration of self-sense. I'll take a brain aneurysm, thank you — just one more headache of a hundred I get on a daily basis, bringing with it finality.

August 20

WATCHED TONIGHT THE CONCLUSION OF THE virtual Democratic Convention that ended with the nominations of Biden for president & Kamala Harris for vice president, and an array of ordinary people offering testaments. Some thoughts. First, while in western cultures stuttering is regarded as idiocy, in others it's considered the sign of a savant. Second, you never outgrow a stutter. What you learn is how to stutter as well as possible. The vowels you have to take a running start for. The consonants where you know your larynx locks up like a machine gun stuck on the same artillery round. Third, no one stutters when they sing. Fourth, I'm unaware of any stutterer who can remember any time in his life when he didn't stutter. So your most apparent flaw does indeed become defining from the first moment of self-consciousness. Fifth, stuttering comes more naturally to you than not stuttering, which means that the rare moments when you don't stutter — when you "overcome" your stutter — are your least authentic. The disordered relationship among your mind & mouth & lungs is your natural order of things, an epilepsy of transmission. Sixth, your speech is gripped by a physicality in which the most casual hello bursts from a knot in the pit of your gut & a constriction of your chest, and with the most perfunctory yes (oh those y's!) comes the feeling of trying to touch something on a very high shelf barely out of reach. Finally, by its very nature a stutter isolates you. From the outset it cuts you off from other kids who tend to be merciless about such things, and people draw conclusions about you that may not be accurate. Surmounting isolation is what the rest of your life is about. You might become someone who locks himself in rooms & writes weird novels. Or more impressively you might have the good humor & courage to go on national TV as a 13-yr-old kid from New Hampshire named Braydon Harrington where you employ your battered young voice on behalf of an important man — maybe the next President of the United States — who bothered to make a connection with you when he didn't have to. Or you might be the man himself giving the speech of his life, acknowledging the minefield & continuing to cross, b/c in this life one Word is worth the humiliation & it is d-d-democracy.

August 21

I DON'T KNOW HOW TO DEAL with anything except write about it. Maybe in my case writing is a perversion, a retreat from life in the name of bearing witness. Writing involves navigating exquisite perspectives — one vantage point is too close, another too far. One is so distant you can't find yourself anymore, another so near you're vanishing up your own nether regions. At that point you can only trust that your instincts were right to begin with, you can only trust that the compass has been showing true north all along however estranged the map. Among those who know me materializes a sense of the untethered man.

Right now everyone in America is a grenade with the pin pulled. Amid echoes of Toplessgate I'm advised to stick to social media posts that are "anodyne," but these days nothing's anodyne. Write "Good morning" and you may get responses to the effect of, "Easy for a West Coast elitist to say. Does it occur to you there are places on the planet right now where it's not morning? That there are places right now where people are living at night?" Withdrawal from social media is itself taken as an act of aggression. I'm gun-shy about everything & nothing is more contemptible than a gun-shy word-slinger.

August 24

SPENT TODAY TAKING MY MOM TO the doctor & then the market, things she can do less & less for herself. I steel myself for…what? An end that comes too soon? A protracted deterioration in which the end doesn't come soon enough? Figures from the past I knew barely well enough to count as forgotten: a woman Viv & I met who produced a cable series for TV…last summer at the beach she saw a small wounded seagull on the sand and, when she went to help, was bitten. From the bite grew some disease that rotted her from the inside till it reached her brain, and she died two weeks later from a literally lethal act of kindness. Or an editor I knew before I was published, decades ago when I stayed at his place on Elizabeth Street south of Houston, reading punk magazines & spying Wm Burroughs outside the front door. What friendship we had foundered on my lack of interest in doing coke with him & another novelist — together the two went on to great success with a novel about novelists & editors doing coke. The editor climbed the ladder of success till recently he was pushed off for a presumably untenable indiscretion. This is what we come to in the end, ungrateful snarls of broken birds & blunt expulsions from our upward trajectories. Are we the first generation confounded by getting old? As every generation before us venerated their elders, were we the first to despise age, so intent were we on staying young? Are we the first to find aging so alienating that we don't know who we are the older we grow?

August 27

How's it possible this happens again? asks the clueless old white guy before the TV. No knee on the neck, just a police officer grabbing an unarmed Black victim by his t-shirt so he can pump seven rounds into the man's back in front of the man's three kids. Do cops ever take a psychological exam more difficult than the cognitive test the President brags about passing, where he had to distinguish between a horse & a can opener? "We love America," a Black basketball coach pleads on TV, "why can't it love us back?"

August 28

Seven years ago I took Zema to see a movie called *42*, the number that Brooklyn Dodger legend Jackie Robinson wore on his jersey & no one else has worn since it was retired in the '90s. Viv & I deliberated fitfully at what point to pull back for Zema the curtain of American racism, and *42* turned out to be an apt choice. It was an heroic story that had something resembling a happy ending while not, at the same time, whitewashing past or present, and at its center was a valiant & larger-than-life figure who, by doing nothing but being great, began a lineage of activist athletes including Ali, Tommie Smith, John Carlos, Kareem, LeBron, Colin Kaepernick. If the right movie was *42*, Chadwick Boseman as Robinson was the right actor b/c his performance, like Robinson himself, threaded a resistance neither reactive nor acquiescent. Boseman remained the right actor right up till he died today on what happens to be Jackie Robinson Day. Only in the mass public consciousness a handful of years, he might have been startled by the nerve his death has touched in the last few hours.

In keeping with the poise he conveyed as Robinson, the actor apparently did his dying of colon cancer privately in plain sight. Boseman also was an electrifying James Brown in *Get On Up* and, oh yeah, he made another pretty good picture called *Black Panther*. It got some attention. Arriving months after white-supremacist torchlit parades in Charlottesville, it had all the more impact as the apex of an emerging African American cinema. In the lead role Boseman, chosen over two dozen contenders, became the face of a moment. Twenty years from now it will be regarded as the most important movie of this decade — more than that, it will be the most American movie of any America still worth believing in. Now Boseman rests in power and they don't get any more gone-too-soon.

September 04

Trump's needy narcissism can't help inserting him
into scenes where it does him no political good. The Trump
campaign strategy makes sense — the more the election is a
referendum on Trump, the worse for him, and the more it's
a choice between Trump & a Biden characterized as at once
senile & radicalized, the better. But the strategy doesn't work
for someone congenitally incapable of letting anyone else be
the focus of attention under any circumstances. The man who
never does anything that isn't in his own interest is too much
who he is to do what's in his own interest.

Over 40 years Trump branded himself, branded his bldgs,
branded his steaks, branded his "university"…in politics he
successfully branded his opponents. So one of the growing ironies
of the moment is that he's become his own worst brand. How
many will go into polling booths over the next two months,
look at the Trump brand on their ballots and, whatever else
they think of the last four years, choose another four of a mania
that grows by the day? There are no gamechangers anymore, no
October surprises that will matter. Is anyone paying attention?
Now the answer is yes.

September 12

A week that was. Temperatures of 120+ degrees,
hottest in recorded L.A. history, comparable to Death Valley.
So where's Oklahoma Senator Jim Inhofe with his fucking

snowball now? Laws of climate unravel with the laws of men. The Attorney General assigns himself the President's case pertaining to rape charges. While trash talking vets who have died for their country, the President dismisses wholesale the current racial reckoning. Released tapes reveal Trump knew how bad the pandemic was seven months ago & concealed it from the public even as doing so killed people. More indications of his financial Russian connections come to light. In the cities 17-yr-olds with AR-15s are driven cross state lines by their moms to shoot BLM marchers. Most stunning: Nothing changes. Polls barely register a tick. My friend Ventura is briefly in town and we lunch outside today at the local bistro for as long as the heat allows. "Those who America has wronged most," he says, "are the only ones who can save it." He makes the outlandish prediction that not only will Trump lose but be impeached again before leaving office.

September 13

MY MOM TURNS 93 IN TWO months and we all should have such a remarkable run. I've decided to stay at her place part-time for her peace of mind as much as anything else. She's very happy to have me here so I'm trying not to be a baby about it, but at this moment I swear I hear a particular "news" network coming from so many TVs in the house it's quadrophonic. As Fox has it, every city in America run by Democrats is now in flames, peopleoid masses of suspicious hues rage in the streets, and cops are slaughtered by "anarchists" faster than they can breathe. My Mom hasn't a doubt in the universe Trump is going to win handily.

September 14

DON'T THINK TOO HIGHLY OF ME — she's my Mom, for God's sake. In an early '80s French picture called *Nuit de Varennes* (one of whose characters is Tom Paine), someone calls writers "a race of spies." So I hope no one thinks I'm spying on a defenseless old woman when in fact that's exactly what I'm doing, and I hope no one thinks I'm turning her into writing fodder when that's also what I'm doing. Like the scorpion said, It's my nature.

I can't think of when I last spent a night here let alone two. Forty years? In the room where I sleep are old photos from her life. My Mom, it can objectively be said, was a good-looking woman in her starlet days when she was among the Colosseum's Romans howling for poor Alan Young's blood in *Androcles and the Lion*. She was on magazine covers vaguely resembling Gene Tierney, a couple shot by my Dad who was a photographer & met my Mom in his Westwood Village studio. Hanging on the walls are certificates from her meditation period signed by the same yogi the Beatles knew, and an award as Granada Hills Citizen of the Year in 1983 for running the local theater. There are two books I always see together — *Atlas Shrugged* & the Holy Bible — while a stray paperback called *Zeroville* props up the TV that broadcasts Fox, Fox, Fox. The first thing I hear this morning is how Obama — oh how Fox pines for him — paid terrorists to kill Israelis. I assume the network means, assuming it means anything that actually means something, when Obama unfroze Iranian assets, which is to say the Iranians' own money, as part of the Iranian treaty that Trump has undone. The Foxsters are supremely confident Biden is going to drool in public for two months, tho cooler heads such as they exist offer cautionary mutterings otherwise. On my Mom's refrigerator are three photos: the 40th President of the United States, the 45th, and me. Ronnie, Donnie & Steve, the three amigos. At the moment nowhere feels like home. Say this for my Mom, she was always a great cook & still is. I sleep a lot.

September 18

A TRUMP SUPPORTER IN FLORIDA IS quoted in the news calling the President "manic, uneducated, illogical, vulgar, amoral, narcissistic...but to those of us who support what he's accomplished, it feels like he's our O.J." Every day we make allowances for the bloody knife. Every day we pretend the glove doesn't fit.

Got home from my Mom's this afternoon and I'm talking to Parker & Zema around the dining room table when the house shakes with a huge crash. I look out our window to see, barely feet away, a crumpled mail truck that's come rolling down the hill above us, demolishing our wooden fence only to be stopped by the retaining wall outside our back door. I mutter to myself, Come on, 2020, is this really the best you got? Within minutes the news delivers the cruel answer that Ruth Bader Ginsburg is dead.

September 19

I'M NO GOOD AT RALLYING CRIES or leading charges, and my depression is past the point of wallow-deep. It's more thrash-hard-as-I-can-not-to-go-under deep. But we don't have the luxury of our despair, we don't have the luxury of resignation. We shouldn't waste the least energy marveling that Mitch McConnell is exactly the nihilist we always knew he was & will ram thru a right-wing Supreme Court justice in five weeks after sitting on a more moderate nomination for 10 months in Obama's final year. I'm barely enough an agnostic to embrace the possibility that she died when she did for a cosmic reason, and I'm barely enough a mystic to embrace the possibility that her dying is a sign for everyone to do one more thing than whatever we've already done. At two in the morning I sign up to be a poll worker on Election Day, pandemic be damned, and starting tomorrow we're regularly sending money to not just Biden but eight Senate candidates. It's not that hard figuring out what she would want & that dying in vain isn't it.

September 26

NOT IDEOLOGY BUT THE WEAPONIZATION OF shamelessness is the most fascist aspect of who we become. We're for whatever we're for at the moment we're for it, for whatever reason we're for it at that moment. The pandemic toll barrels toward a quarter million dead as the administration argues in court against the right of people with pre-existing conditions to have health insurance. As Justice Ginsburg is buried, the President nominates to her seat a woman with scant judicial experience who reportedly served as a "handmaid" in a religious coven. Trump finally says explicitly what we all know — that the only result he'll accept on Election Day is one in which he's the winner.

This afternoon Viv & Zema drive up the canyon highway heading home when, before their eyes, a snake slithers up from under the hood of the car onto the windshield. It would be cooler for the purposes of this journal if it had happened to me, but if it had happened to me there wouldn't be a journal, b/c if any fucking snake slithers up my fucking windshield I'm running the car off the road into the 100-ft drop below. As with Winston & rats in *1984*, snakes are my Room 101. Coolly Viv pulled the car over to the roadside & waited as the snake — nonplussed in its own fashion — leapt to the low branch of an overhead tree. If snakes coming out of the car isn't an End Days omen, I don't know what is, but Viv points out they're good luck in Native American culture.

September 29

THE PRESIDENTIAL "DEBATE" TONIGHT BETWEEN TRUMP & Biden as "moderated" by hapless Fox anchor Chris Wallace is the most spectacular clusterfuck in modern American politics. The President's clear intent is to sabotage the event in every way. This is 48 hrs after a *New York Times* exposé revealed Trump lost huge sums of money over the decades, paid less per-capita tax than any American alive, deducted $70k haircuts & his "fame" as a commodity worth hundreds of thousands of dollars while marveling aloud at the IRS's stupidity, and is in hock half a billion dollars to Turks slaughtering Syrians, Arabs dismembering American journalists & Russians laundering money thru Deutsche Bank. Watching the debate I decide if there's any actual strategy to the President's disruption it's to try & make Biden stutter, throwing off any natural groove that might constitute a speech pattern. "Would you shut up, man?" — muttered by Biden under his breath with a shake of his head — already becomes a meme.

October 02

TOO MUCH HAPPENS TOO FAST TO keep up with. America exhausts the language of its telling. Increasingly there's reason to believe the President has lost his mind…or is it simply that his madness reaches new rubicons beyond old rubicons? Recent twitter tirades sound disturbed even by his standard — tacitly he approves the plan of a dozen lunatics to kidnap & execute the female governor of Michigan. Serious conversations rage inside government & out as to what can be done. Half of America will vote for him.

The news broke right before I was going to bed, keeping me up another hour, and this morning it's all over every paper & TV around the world: The President & First Lady have Covid. For 48 hrs everyone in his circle knew they had the virus even as Trump attended the debate with Biden & held rallies with hundreds of people & went on lying as he has for six months about the single greatest national security threat since 9/11. He no longer figuratively shoots people on Fifth Avenue. Literally he wages biological warfare.

October 11

BEGUN ONLINE SEVERAL YEARS AGO WITH a growing number of supporters in Congress, a conspiracy mothership called QAnon cobbles bits of Scientology & bargain-basement *Manchurian Candidate*, asserting the country is run by a satanic sect of pedophiles including Obama, Hillary Clinton, Tom Hanks, Ellen DeGeneres, Katy Perry, German Chancellor Angela Merkel whose secret grandfather was Hitler, and the assassins of Princess Diana avenging her efforts to thwart 9/11. QAnon prepares to launch the Storm, an uprising that will take care of these folks in a fell swoop. Supporters include Fox's Sean Hannity, radio psycho Alex Jones, screw-loose has-been TV actor Roseanne Barr, proudly racist Iowa congressman Steve King, the Nosferatu of American politics Rudy Giuliani, this year's Republican Senate nominee from Oregon, this year's Republican Senate nominee from Delaware who also believes the earth is flat, a Republican congressional nominee from Georgia, another Republican congressional nominee from Colorado, the entire hierarchy of the Republican Party in Texas, and the President himself regarded by QAnon as a godlike führer called Q+. The FBI identifies QAnon as a potential terrorist organization. Clearly these people are dangerous, but the aesthete in me can't help nervously admiring the creative berserkitude, and the libertarian in me can't help noting just how much craziness short of actual violence the Constitution is bound to protect....

I realize that by celebrating every new Republican Covid revelation — by which virtually the entire Trump government comes down with the virus — I'm not just flirting with Karma but ravishing her beneath the staircase.

October 15

VIV & I ARE IN THE last round of mediation, which slowed during the spring & summer as everyone was quarantined. Otherwise things have gone smoothly over Zoom in our garage. There remains some confusion as to what to do with the house & when to do it. On the one hand we want to disrupt Zema's life as little as possible while she's in high school. On the other hand there can be no question: Sooner or later the fires are coming to Topanga. Even now the whole West Coast is in flames again. It's taken a couple weeks but the East Coast media finally takes note. "Oh, look. Smoke."

October 17

I GET A CALL FROM SOMEONE in my Mom's Bible-study group. One of the 12 women in the group has Covid. The women sit inside a room in a circle without masks. "Why?" demands my Mom's doctor when I take her to see him. She likes him — he's a heartthrob of Eastern European or Middle

Eastern descent, the sort of doctor you see on TV. Today, tho, he's annoyed. "I hate the mask," she retorts. "We all hate the masks," he answers back, "but this thing is real and, at your age especially, it's serious." I like the "this thing is real" b/c lately Mom has been wondering aloud if it's overblown. She's floated arguments she hears on Fox & from the President that the masks don't do anything. The doctor sends us to a center where a test — a swab up the nose — produces a result in half an hour. We're both negative.

Friends inform me social media is swept by a rumor that I'm having a torrid affair with the latina Brontë who came to my defense during Toplessgate.

October 21

NEGATIVE TEST OR NO, THERE ARE times I'm convinced I have it. Or my body is convinced even as my mind knows better. Or my mind is a liar, or maybe I've got the flu. As more reports come out, the virus expresses itself variably...any part of the body that receives blood, which is to say every part of the body, can be affected in the form of diabetes, glaucoma.... Some people die from it, some people don't die but never really get better, some people have it & never know. It's a science-fiction virus, a shapeshifting chameleon disease adapting to the host system, capriciously deciding if it wants to thrive off that system or kill it.

A third of the country believes there's no disease at all. Assuming he's indeed recovered from Covid, the President again insists it's nothing, also claiming to personally have discovered a cure. Tonight the First Lady, barely seen in weeks, cancels an appearance with the President on the campaign trail, and here's the telling thing: If she were to die, does any reasonable person doubt Trump would cover it up? Does anyone doubt what choice he'd make between his reelection & the life of his teenage son? On what rational basis can anyone doubt the worst of a President who, according to a report tonight, deliberately orphaned 545+ latinx kids, hijacking them from their parents as a punitive measure & then purposely losing track of them? It would be bad enough if this were incompetence. Rather it's a plan forged with calculation by Trump with his former Attorney General — who Trump later fired for not being debased enough — to make coming to America as horrible as possible for as many people as possible. The cost of one American dream: your child....

The President demands that the current Attorney General arrest Biden, Biden's son & Obama. Yesterday Trump stormed out of a *60 Minutes* interview furious at the journalist's questions.

October 28

FIVE DAYS LEFT OF VOTING & there's new dread — or resurgent old dread — of Trump voters who don't reveal themselves to pollsters. I get an email from the Los Angeles County Registrar Recorder. *Thank you for your interest in serving as a worker in the presidential election. The County Clerk is no longer recruiting election workers. We encourage you to apply in future elections.*

October 30

THIS AFTERNOON ON THE FIRST DAY when polls open in the canyon, I vote at the Mermaid Café, a speakeasy almost a century ago. It's as calm as you'd expect a place called the Mermaid Café in Topanga to be, in contrast with new reporting that fully three quarters of the electorate anticipate violence around the election and, should Trump lose, no peaceful transfer of power. This would be unprecedented but for President-elect Lincoln smuggling himself into Washington in disguise by secret train in Feb 1861, and it's as unprecedented as a plague that, in the 100 hrs between now & the election deadline, will infect 100k people per day with someone dying every minute & a half, with half a million deaths in sight by Inauguration Day.

I have nothing new to add. I realize this hasn't stopped me before. I'm sure whatever I say bears repeating by someone less full of himself and more original & insightful & eloquent. We've all been in the thick of this so long it's easy to forget in these final days something historically momentous is about to happen, a defining event like early July 1863 leading up to & including Gettysburg, the election of 1864 & the six months that followed, the election of 1932, the first months of 1942, the last half of October 1962, September 11, 2001. When the voting is over Tues night, whether we know the outcome then or the day after or the next week or month, one of three things certainly will be true: The country will have repudiated trumpism in convincing fashion, or the country will have lurched fully into trumpian authoritarianism, or the country will remain divided into two Americas irreconciled. That some Americans of good faith will vote for the President won't change how his victory vindicates bad faith. That some Americans of good faith will vote against the President won't change the trumpism that means to erase any America that could elect Trump's predecessor.

The country may be complicated but this election isn't: We're Trump, or Not. This has meant the forging among us of unlikely alliances, the setting aside of skirmishes in order to bear together a larger crucible, the acknowledgment that two choices & only two is the arithmetic that saves the country. No independent candidates or green candidates or libertarian candidates, no reform candidates or populist candidates or federalist candidates, no progressive candidates or peace & freedom candidates or guns & dope candidates or workers' world candidates or Randian objectivist candidates, or know-nothing candidates or head-so-far-up-your-ass-just-so-you-can-see-how-dark-it-really-gets candidates, or whatever exotic bullshit self-identification that one's ego desires or one's so-called conscience deigns to accept. It won't matter whether we have treason in our hearts. This is a moment when self-indulgence is its own treason, for which one answers to the God of Math who's muse to the Goddess of History. Math never sleeps. Character is destiny, said the Greek philosopher Heraclitus — a romantic, I guess, asserting that sooner or later the good guy wins. Should the President be reelected we'll be complicit in the murder of a faith without which this country in particular is nothing. Repudiate or ratify, deliverance or defeat. Utopiate later, save democracy now. One final vote one final time for the better angels. We hear whose name they whisper & whose they don't.

November 2020 – January 2021

As a nation of free men, we must live through all time or die by suicide.

Lincoln

Election Eve

SPENDING THE NIGHT AT MY MOM'S. Tomorrow morning I'll walk her to the polls so she can cancel out my vote. Fox "News" glows from the TV like the mystery box in *Kiss Me Deadly*.

Most interesting guy I've met in my travels cross Fox Nation is Mark Levin. Listen to Levin awhile & it's clear that, singularly among Fox nincompoops like Steve Doocy whose brains wouldn't fill a shot glass, in no way is Levin stupid. There's erudition in his arguments. He has several law degrees that appear to have been received with distinction, and he was chief of staff 30 yrs ago for the Attorney General. But Levin is an unhappy man. He hates us. He...hates...us. He believes we're a "mob" determined to destroy America, which is to say he believes about me what I believe about him. First time I heard Levin was on an ad for his radio show where, with a gay mince, he mimicked libtards running down America over their cappuccinos. "Don't you just hate this country?" He's filled with rage & would drop me from that same airplane from which I'd drop his heroes (tho not him) b/c I'm filled with rage too. I ponder the possibility that over the past year & a half I've become my own Mark Levin.

Election Day

AND SUDDENLY WE'RE HERE. ON THE way back to the canyon I stop at the pharmacy, refill my lexapro, get to my house, proceed directly upstairs, do not pass Hello How Are You, do not collect Nice To Have You Home, climb into bed head first, dig my way to Tarkovsky's Room at the center of the Zone, hide in my bunker at the end of the world beyond texts, emails & memory, and wait till it's over.

November 04

NOTHING IS RESOLVED. *REPUDIATE OR RATIFY* — but America does neither. First returns are shitty. Trump leads in both popular & electoral votes. So far America is as red as the bloody asterisk itself. Given Trump's effort to delegitimize the result before it's final, how does faith in our system survive? Moreover, why should it? How does faith in the American Idea survive? Moreover, why should it? Does the idea exist at all anymore? Does faith?

November 05

BECAUSE OF THE NUMBER OF VOTES cast — the most ever & the highest percentage in more than a century — and with the stakes so great, the tally is careful. Without waiting for a final count, Republicans file lawsuits contesting results on the trumpian grounds that they don't like them. Biden votes are illegal by definition & the count should have halted when the President was ahead. Trump has sued his way out of problems his whole life b/c suits compel settlements. It's unclear whether he understands this isn't a real estate deal.

November 06

STILL NO CONCLUSION TO THE PRESIDENTIAL race. Matters hang in the balance in four states. The sense of national exhaustion is flagrant.

November 07

WAKE AT 5:30. A LITTLE PAST six there's a cloudburst, forceful & lasting no longer than 10 mins. Toss & turn in bed till seven when I dress & head to the local café to get coffee for me, Viv, the kids. First day of 2020 that feels autumnal — cool & sharp. Back home I build the first fire since the early spring of the pandemic. I'm slightly disappointed the girl at the café got my order wrong — a latte instead of an effete cappuccino in honor of Mark Levin. I sit by the fire & am just settling into work when, at 8:24, the announcement flashes across my laptop that Joe Biden & Kamala Harris are President- & Vice-President-elect.

[later that afternoon]

CHURCH BELLS ACROSS PARIS RING IN the waning twilight. London night skies fill with fireworks. Covid or not, the world has a block party. Planetary reaction to Trump's defeat is euphoric — relief that America isn't quite terminal after all, just critical. American streets explode joyfully all day & into the dark, with international correspondents comparing it to countries where dictators fall. Conspicuous in the interviews with random celebrants is how often *her* name comes up, how often *she* is the image on the signs people carry.

Of course everyone loves Joe. He had the savvy & largeness of character — after she skewered him in early debates when she was still a presidential contender — to choose her. But if the only instance in vaguely recent history of a vice-presidential nominee making a difference to the final result is Lyndon Johnson in 1960, anecdotal evidence to any honest pair of ears & eyes is that, for a significant number of voters, Kamala sealed the deal. Seeing Biden & Harris together this evening onstage, anyone would be struck by how much sense it makes, the senior statesman with the experience to set aright the ship of state, side by side with the future. Of course I'm getting ahead of myself, but who can persuasively rule out the possibility we're seeing not just the 46th President but the 47th?

November 08

LISTENING TO BIDEN LAST NIGHT GIVE his first address as President-elect, I wondered if Make-Do Joe — who we all sort of settled for — might be exactly the right guy in the right place at the right time. Now under the new President, it's up to all of us to leave aside rancor & show generosity of spirit. We need to learn how to listen to each other. With malice toward none & charity for...oh screw this. Fuck your feelings, trumptards. When Trump concedes, or when one of these Republican hacks offers Biden a simple congratulations, then I'll drag my magnanimity out from the bottom drawer of my soul. Till then, little kids in cages still won't see their parents again.

November 10

SYMBOLOGY RAGES SO HEAVILY THAT YOU would strike it from a novel. Biden receives exactly the number of electoral votes Trump got four years ago. He's the 46th President — his son Beau, for whom the father ran this race, died at the age of 46. The state that delivers the presidency is Pennsylvania, both Biden's home state & the Republic's….

The only President since the 1880s to have lost the popular vote twice, Trump receives 11 million more votes than he got in 2016 — the one thing that, in my naïveté, I would flatly have predicted against. Politics is capricious but caprice isn't the same as a fluke & few things in American politics are flukes, including Trump's presidency.

November 11

HAVE I MENTIONED I'VE NEVER MET a buzz I couldn't kill? Trump remains the manifestation of our rot. He fully eclipses Reagan, Eisenhower & Teddy Roosevelt not to mention Lincoln in the Republican consciousness. Barely retaining control, Democrats lose ground in the House of Representatives. Would it have made a difference if Speaker Pelosi pursued impeachment more boldly rather than under the radar in the most limited terms possible? Nuts-and-bolts brilliant, she's big-picture myopic, no more so than when it came to a Covid relief pkg on Election Eve.

In the Senate, Democrats win two battleground states but lose half a dozen. Unless seven weeks from now they can take two seats in a Georgia runoff — a long shot — then in a Senate where not a single Republican acknowledges Biden's election, Mitch McConnell remains Majority Leader, providing no reason for assuming he won't do to Biden as he did to Obama. Trumpism inexorably evolves into its own American fascism that's part populism, part racism & part economic despair too ignorant to direct its legitimate fury at the powerful rather than the powerless. America dodges a bullet but fails to redeem its soul.

November 20

IN THE NINE WEEKS BEFORE THE Constitution fires him, retaining command of the military & access to nuclear codes & mechanisms of executive power, facing post-presidency indictments in New York from which he can't protect himself with a federal pardon, Trump torches American governance. He does it in the courts, on the phone, from his limo gliding thru crowds of supporters. Having badgered the Attorney General to arrest the President's political opponent & the President's predecessor, the President now tries coercing state legislators into overturning the election. Dumbfounding is how this dumbfounds no one. At the same time, a world plague has augmented itself in ascending multiples afflicting the President, First Lady, two of the President's sons, the presidential

Chief of Staff & National Security Adviser, none of it to any effect in terms of any of them caring anything about any other American alive or dead....

There's a God after all and this is what She wreaks. As Lincoln noted in his second inaugural, Americans have gotten the equation wrong from the beginning. The question has never been whether God is on our side but whether we're on God's. Nobody believes Trump won reelection unless she or he chooses to. Trumpism's refusal to be persuaded differently leaves only the option of vanquishing it thoroughly, with its supporters dying soon enough for our country & children to survive them. Empathize with these voters no more. Stupidity drips from their fingers in the blood of American stigmata, not holes in their hands but slits in our wrists.

November 25

AH 2020. CAN IT GET ANY better? Our house already is in transition anticipating my departure, movers coming this morning to relocate a dresser downstairs, the dead TV upstairs heading to the dump along with the sofa that the dogs have barfed on for 10 yrs. The day, in other words, began in benign chaos, and only by this evening began to calm when, sitting in the bedroom upstairs trying to figure out insurance policies, I hear a sound approximating the start of an airline at takeoff.

"The house is on fire, the house is on fire!" I hear Viv shout. Downstairs the fireplace has gone up in a gust of flame. Reality is a clumsy poet — could the irony be more tortured? Evacuate a week for a fire that never happens only so a year later a sudden inferno in the fireplace can threaten to burn the house down under our feet. While my frantic brain tries to figure out in what order to push the numbers 9, 1 & 1 on my cell, Viv grabs a fire extinguisher & puts the fire out. The kids move stuff out of the house that's now swallowed in soot. Marriage aside, it's a hell of a family. The fire department arrives mins later.

Pandemic Thanksgiving

IF COVID DIDN'T KILL OFF THE holiday, a house of smoke this morning finishes the job, capping weeks of snakes crawling out of the car & mail trucks tumbling down the hill. Where are all your pretentious metaphors about democracy now, Erickson? We spend the day dragging the rest of the house's contents outside. The dead fireplace lies in the backyard in a heap of scrap metal where the firefighters left it. Viv & I are trying to avoid a fight when Zema steps in, summoning every bit of Abyssinian wisdom to coolly de-escalate the situation & speak of trauma, tension, keeping our cool & other mysteries of the cosmos. I marvel at my kids: a Dalai Lama for a son & future United Nations Secretary General for a daughter. Thanksgiving dinner is take-out Mediterranean chicken.

December 03

ZEMA HOLDS A DIM VIEW OF capitalism as any thoughtful 15-yr-old will these days. This isn't a matter of philosophy but experience. What's capitalism done for her generation except put them a quarter million dollars in debt getting thru college so they can work at Coffee Bean? On Fox, Mark Levin repeats the word "Marxism" as an incantation, but it means nothing to a future American electorate. Zema argues that in the DNA of even regulated capitalism is a greed which, by its nature, rejects regulation — pretty smart argument. I don't disagree with her, only suggesting that in the '50s a regulated capitalism created the greatest middle class of all time, to which she responds, "For white people." Viv chortles later, "You walked into that one." The single point I score is that socialism is an impossible political brand in America & will remain so for a time to come — even Bernie-supporter Parker now concedes only Biden could have won this election. But the aging Levins are on borrowed time. Capitalism displays the incompetence & inflexibility that swallowed Soviet communism in the '80s, and if capitalists want to save it from devouring itself, they better find a way damn quick. Just tossing around the word Marxism isn't going to cut it. The aging Erickson is on borrowed time, too — this won't be the last argument he loses to his kids.

Today the President pardons the former two-week National Security Adviser who led "Lock her up!" chants against Hillary Clinton while selling out his country. In turn Michael Flynn calls on Trump to dismiss the election result & declare martial law. Fox's *The Five*, barely adding up among them to one thinking adult, are in a tizzy about California's governor imposing social-distance mandates that he then stupidly violated. *The Five's* revolving membership includes "comedian" Greg Gutfeld, who always seizes on liberal hypocrisy as an object lesson not in liberal hypocrisy but flawed policy. If the town mayor puts a red light at Elm & Maple to curb accidents and then himself runs the red light, Gutfeld will argue this shows what's wrong with red lights. Too stupid to be alive, you can never be too stupid for TV.

December 08

AT THE URGING OF EVERYONE INCLUDING Viv & my Mom, I get out of town as the entire state of California closes down. On a gorgeous gusty day I head up the pandemic highway that once belonged to Spanish kings. Santa Barbara is a ghost town. Stay in Cambria tonight at a motel where they upgrade me to their best room with a view of the ocean. I resist the temptation to watch the news.

December 10

GOT INTO MONTEREY LAST NIGHT BY way of Big Sur. Today Ventura & I walk a coast that he describes as a "psychic vortex," the westernmost land mass that pulled in Spanish sailors. For a guy more apocalyptic than I, he's more optimistic about Trumpism: "This fog will lift."

December 12

THIS MORNING I'M AT A BEST Western in Arroyo Grande. Yesterday three quarters of the states that went Republican &

a majority of Republicans in the House of Representatives call for overturning the biggest election in American history. 2020's singular political revelation is that more & more Americans aren't merely weary of democracy but hostile to it. Last night as I was pulling into the motel, news flashed across my phone that the Supreme Court ruled against Trump 9-0, albeit with legalistic caveats from the Court's two most conservative members.

This was followed by a call from Texas Republicans for secession. A rare Republican voice of conscience, an Illinois Congressman named Adam Kinzinger, answers in a statement, "My guy Lincoln already told you no." You can research the rash of recent anti-Lincoln literature published by right-wing authors whose names I'm not going to promote here, but why not take my word for it? Have I led you so wrong so far? Of course trumpism prefers Trump to Lincoln — how would it not? What is it about Lincoln that doesn't offend trumpist sensibility? America struggles to breathe a particularly exquisite faith without which it strangles on the snot of its nihilism, engendering a particularly American amorality in the name of patriotism. There's that word again that the rest of us allowed them to take from us. We need to rediscover our inner patriots who break down at a testament worth our tears, so long as we distinguish it from a reality worth our rage.

December 14

BACK IN L.A. TODAY AS THE pro-forma convocation of the Electoral College advances Biden & Harris to their elected positions, American politics are more balkanized than any time since Reconstruction. The Left fractures between liberal centrism that's sometimes bereft of nerve & progressivism that's sometimes bereft of sense — when you have to explain to people that "defund the police" doesn't mean defunding the police, it's a problem. The trumpist Right fractures from schisms within Fox Nation whose business model wants to abandon Trump but whose market won't allow it. A quarter million are dead from the pandemic with another quarter million new cases per day, but ironically the President's half of the country has no interest in his one true success — the development of a vaccine — b/c he led them to believe there's no need for a vaccine in the first place.

December 15

TODAY IS THE SINGLE STRANGEST ENTRY in this journal b/c not a single strange thing happened. I answer emails. I write a column. I have a headache. I go to the dentist for a crown. I pick up the dogs from the vet. The family gets a Christmas tree. Every single thing is ordinary. Not a single thing isn't ordinary. A FedEx plane doesn't crash in our backyard. A rain of lizards doesn't pelt our house. No one on social media accuses me of necrophilia. Aztec Brontë, with whom I'm supposedly having an affair, posts on social media a photo of Ingmar Bergman, so maybe she has a thing for moody Swedes after all.

Pandemic Christmas

AS LAST NEW YEAR FELT LESS like New Year than any preceding New Year, so feels this Christmas even with Viv's valiant efforts at decorating the house & cooking the Christmas French toast that my Mom used to make. In many ways the day is pleasant, especially with the kids. But sitting at the table I realize this is the last Christmas of this family in this form. A year from now my Mom either won't be here or won't be the same person, and a week from now Viv won't be my wife.

December 26

THIS MORNING VIV WAKES TO NEWS that her older brother is seriously ill in the hospital, not with Covid but cancer. This unspeakable year barely had the decency to wait till Christmas was over. A week left of 2020, then rip it from the calendar & carve it on a tombstone —

Pandemic New Year

A CONFLICTED & UNSETTLING BEGINNING TO 2021 full of mixed omens & old business from the year before. Over the past week the President has pardoned nearly 30 people, no sleaze or criminality unrewarded so long as it was committed on his behalf. Two Senate runoffs in slowly purpling Georgia take place between now & certification by Congress of the Electoral College result. That same day the President calls for his supporters to converge on Washington for the blunt purpose of overthrowing a constitutional election — this after eight weeks of spending millions of dollars on recounts that widened rather than narrowed Biden's lead, with nearly five dozen courts finding against the President's "case" or dismissing it entirely.

Per our mediation agreement, this also is the day that Viv & I are no longer married after 24 yrs. All this is overshadowed by confirmation this morning that Viv's brother is dying from a kidney cancer more advanced than anyone knew. The hospital in Grand Rapids has helplessly discharged him and he's returned to his beautiful lakeside house where tonight he lies in bed facing the water he loves. Lots of good things happened at that house while I was part of this family — balmy summer cookouts & snowy Christmas dinners. Pure Americana at its richest. Not clear how long Randy has. Viv last got a text from him a month ago. A former ship captain, he signed off as always, "I wish you fair seas."

January 03

DROP OFF VIV AT LAX FOR a midnight flight to Michigan, a decision made scarcely two hours ago. Last night her brother seemed to have a matter of weeks. Now he deteriorates so quickly that, after vacillating in the face of the pandemic, Viv decides she has to go, swathed in three masks & a face shield. Tomorrow Randy receives last rites.

January 04

7:30 IN THE MORNING AND I wake to the msg that by the time Viv reached her connecting flight in Detroit, her brother was gone.

January 05

TONIGHT I TAKE A BATH & go to bed early b/c I ache every-where, and when Viv texts that she feels the same, we both conclude we have Covid. But in her case it's the emotions of the 36 hrs since she got to Michigan, arriving at her brother's house as his body was being taken away while her mom wept — I can't bring myself to think of losing my son. In my case the aches are from the physical I had yesterday & side effects of a shingles vaccination. I'm also 15 lbs overweight, two inches shorter than I used to be, due for a colonoscopy, and for the first time in my life have blood pressure high enough to medicate.

Georgia run-off for two Senate seats was today. Democrats have to sweep to take the Senate.

January 07

THIRTY-SIX HOURS SINCE MY LAST ENTRY. Went to bed late last night — about 4½ hrs ago — and woke 30 mins ago to widespread calls for the President's impeachment, immediate resignation, or constitutional removal by the Cabinet. Yesterday was one of those days that swallows up months & years around it. People will write whole books about yesterday. Other major news like Biden's selection for Attorney General — Merrick Garland, cheated out of a Supreme Court seat 5 yrs ago by McConnell — will be footnotes, and the unexpected capture of the United States Senate by Democrats thanks to Georgia, of all states, will wait its turn too....

Upon the ceremonial occasion of Congress certifying the clear electoral victories of Biden & Harris, yesterday the Congressional rotunda was seized by thousands of goons, criminals, hoodlums & terrorists storming security, smashing windows, battering down doors, overwhelming police, ransacking offices, trampling the House & Senate floors & desecrating history, pissing & shitting on the grounds. Dressed in fatigues, camouflage, militia gear & sweats emblazoned *Camp Auschwitz*, carrying QAnon & MAGA signs and armed with automatic weapons & molotov cocktails, the marauders streamed thru the Capitol searching for the Speaker of the House ("Where's Nancy?") as well as the Vice President, who just had stated his intention to formally announce from the Senate podium, as is his designated role, Biden's victory. Now the mob chanted "Hang Mike Pence!" as a noose swung from the porticoes of the outer plaza. Senators & representatives desperately hurried to clandestine security spaces & huddled under desks with the lights off, from which they texted goodbye messages to loved ones & instructions where to locate their final wills. The last time such a threat was posed to Congress was September 11, 2001, with United Airlines 93 commandeered by al-Qaeda &

bound for the Capitol as a bomb before passengers gave their lives to bring the plane down in Pennsylvania.

Televised round the world, the rampage went on for hours at the incessant instigation of the President by way of tweet & video for the past two months & with a morning rally at the Ellipse that circles the White House's south side. There the congregation carried signs reading BRING DC TO ITS KNEES as assorted Trumps & Rudy Giuliani exhorted the assembled troops to "trial by combat." Following the release of taped presidential threats to the Georgia Secretary of State if 11k votes weren't "found" in order to overturn November's verdict — the desperation in Trump's voice is evident — the President insisted to the crowd he won by a landslide. "They rigged it like they never rigged an election before," he went on, "we'll never give up, we'll never concede. We fight. We fight like hell. We'll never take back our country with weakness. If you don't fight like hell, you're not going to have a country anymore. So we're going to walk down Pennsylvania Avenue to the Capitol and I'll be there with you…I love Pennsylvania Avenue," after which he went nowhere but home to watch on TV with satisfaction what he wrought, even as he was futilely beseeched by staff & pols & even some family to call off the melee. Law enforcement roused itself with somewhat less enthusiasm than it brought to the President's Bible photo-op outside the White House seven months ago.

The Congressional certification process recommenced after six hrs once the bldg was finally secured. Five people died &

two bombs were found & dismantled. As the i was dotted & the t was crossed in *democratic*, opposition to the United States Constitution was distilled to Republican congressmen & a White House that literally went dark, disappearing into the night like an evil Brigadoon. Since then, one social media platform after another has cut the President's accounts. This morning the salient images from yesterday involve flags — including the parading of the American swastika otherwise known as the Confederate banner — hoisted thru the people's house, and new confederates scaling rotunda walls to replace the Stars & Stripes with a flag reading TRUMP in case anyone has any confusion about the priorities. One thing you can't accuse these people of is duplicity. They keep telling us who they are while Biden, in an address of indisputably presidential sobriety, insists, "This doesn't represent who we are." Is he sure?

January 08

VIV'S BROTHER IS LAID TO REST next to his father with a ceremony on Lake Michigan — buried by land, remembered by sea.

January 10

EVEN AFTER THE IMPEACHMENT OF A year ago, after the pandemic, after Black Lives Matter & Trump's derision of soldiers stupid enough to die for their country, even after the election & its tortured tallying, this week was of a consequence that tests the limits of mere recitation let alone narrative. The next 10 days will reveal for how much of America the events of the 6th were finally the moment Donald Trump overplayed his hand. The next 10 days will reveal for how much of America the 6th was bloody liberation, an American Kristallnacht as an Austrian-born former California Governor put it — a comparison that flitted across my mind as well which, for once, I dismissed as overly feverish.

For the second time the House will impeach the President not b/c anything practical comes of it but, as was the case a year ago, more than ever history calls for bearing witness. "I don't want to start an argument," my Mom asks in the car, an anguished expression on her face, "but why do they want to impeach him again?" such being the quality of "information" she receives from her favorite news channel named after a glorified hyena. Even my Mom knows Trump didn't win the election let alone by a landslide. "Because he incited an insurrection that killed five people in order to overthrow democracy," I answer. She gasps when I recount Rudy's "trial by combat" words.

January 12

JFK ONCE SAID THE PROBLEM WITH riding the tiger is, sooner or later, you wind up inside the tiger. In the next 36 hrs Trump will become the only President in history impeached twice. Somewhere the ghosts of former Worst-President-Ever contenders James Buchanan, Andrew Johnson & Richard Nixon crack open a bottle. Meanwhile the argument against impeachment, as mounted by Republicans who have torn apart the country, is that it will tear apart the country.

January 13

THE PRESIDENT IS IMPEACHED.

January 14

FOUR IMPEACHMENTS IN AMERICAN HISTORY & half are Trump's. Ventura's prediction of a few months ago has come to pass....

Spent the day looking for somewhere to live. Scoured studios from Toluca Lake to mid-Wilshire to Koreatown. As I drive around the city, the number of homeless camps materializing just in the last couple years is staggering. They're everywhere — under overpasses, on traffic islands, at street corners. Could all these people have come from anywhere else but places they called home not long ago? The rest of us are as much an affront to them as they are to us, and all of us are an affront to any sense of civilization commonly held by a moral people. How many of the new homeless are sick? How many of the camps reflect pockets of the only kind of virus that can challenge a national greed by which we measure what makes America "great again"? Tonight I pick up Viv at LAX returning from Michigan. As upon her departure she arrives in protective gear, a uniformed soldier of the Covid Wars. On the ride home she sits in the car's backseat with both of us wearing masks. Randy's death sinks in.

January 18

THIS PAST WEEKEND AS MOVERS EVACUATE the Trumps from the White House, the President's numbers finally show signs of faltering. It only took abducting children, slandering ethnicities, sundering treaties, auctioning national security, cratering the national economy, ravaging the Constitution, a pandemic killing half a million Americans & a violent siege on the Capitol by turncoats, paramilitarists, white supremacists & anti-Semites. Now two days before the inauguration Fortress America is an intermittent 3k-mile war zone bracing for armed mobs at every capitol in the country. Photos from within the Capitol display soldiers & National Guard sleeping beneath the rotunda's statuary. As the shock of the 6th grows more than wears off, 10 Republicans in Congress vote for impeachment to much media clucking about the "bipartisan" vote. I'm glad for the 10 votes & credit them but remain unimpressed — 10 Republicans out of 200+? More information emerges indicating the Capitol's storming was an inside job, that Republican congressmen & -women provided reconnaissance & access to sedition leaders scoping out the Capitol's tangle of tunnels & entries, that even under siege some Republicans inside texted to the terrorists the Speaker's whereabouts. Prosecutors & the Justice Dept indicate that some of the seditionists meant to function as an execution squad. Keeping in mind that when the looting was over Republicans went back out onto the House floor & voted against democracy, we might conclude some are guilty of intent to commit treason. The problem with living thru these last four yrs & writing this journal these last 18 months is I've so used up by now any & every expression of revulsion as to leave me in a state of mute odium. I could crash my laptop looking for words. There has to be a secret thesaurus hidden deep in the machine's catacombs with language no one's heard.

January 20

AT NOON, WHICH IS TO SAY nine in the morning my time — following a somberly gorgeous ceremony on the promenade last night honoring the plague's victims — Joseph Biden & Kamala Harris become President & Vice President in an inauguration that clings to hope. Lady Gaga gives a defiant rendition of the national anthem. A 22-yr-old black woman named Amanda Gorman knocks out the country as its young poet laureate; as it happens, or maybe it's not happenstance, reportedly she's a stutterer, and b/c no one stutters when she sings, her reading has a mesmerizing musicality about it. If she's the voice of America to come, we may make it after all. Harris is the first woman & person of color to assume the second most powerful position in the land & be a heartbeat from the Presidency. Biden gives a speech that doesn't aspire to be Lincolnesque or Kennedyesque or Rooseveltian or Obamanian but Bidenesque — perfect for the moment b/c it means not to soar but tell things straight & true. Obama is in the audience, George W., the Clintons, even Pence. A minuet of sun & clouds casts shine & shadow on all the faces. No one storms the Capitol or any of the state capitols.

It all makes me so happy as to almost wipe out four years — almost but not quite, of course, because it's all postscript to the day's true event for which I set my alarm early but sleep thru anyway. I wanted to wake in time to see *him* go. I wanted to wake in time to see *him* get on that chopper or plane & never come the fuck back. I wanted to watch the wretched man lumber toward his fate and to imagine prosecutors on the other end waiting to take him into custody, tho I know that won't happen — to imagine INTERPOL seizing him on the other end of an international flight & hauling him off to the Hague, tho that won't happen either. Have I become my own Mark Levin? Whatever else I've been over the course of my life, I've not been a hateful person, and I hate that the now ex-President made me one.

This is the 10-year anniversary of so-called "birtherism" as not just a slander but strategy. It was 10 yrs ago on a morning talk-show that this faux-Manhattan-mogul offered the baseless & racist-to-its-core theory that the first African American President wasn't a real President & wasn't a real American, subsequent to which some months later that President — who might have been on an auction block on the Mississippi River 170 yrs ago — made a laughing-stock of the fuming mogul at a correspondents' dinner, and subsequent to which a quarter century of growing Republican authoritarianism was fused with one humiliated man's quest for vengeance. In the Republican refusal over the last decade to quash birtherism lies trumpism's inevitability & the Republican Party's bankruptcy & everything that happened these last two weeks & these last four years. So yet again…yet again everything comes down to a white racism so blindingly livid we would nearly welcome the asterisk's red blot of blood just for distraction.

Is anyone still paying attention, or has it become impossible to know anymore what to pay attention to? Surely by now, if nothing else, at long last we can finally set aside discussions of "norms." At long last we can set aside bloodless laments for what's normal & what's not, what's "normalized" & what isn't. Maybe now is neither nearly too soon nor quite too late to argue instead what's right & good. We could argue not whether white supremacy is normal but whether it's right & good. We could argue not whether mockery of the weak is normal but whether it's right & good. We could argue whether Arab princes murdering American journalists is right & good, whether the state kidnapping kids from terrorized families seeking asylum is right & good. We could argue whether indifference to assaulted women for the sake of a Supreme Court seat is right & good. We could argue whether suppression of the Native American vote in North Dakota or the African American vote in Georgia is right & good. We could argue, with greater intensity every passing moment, whether we are a nation right & good. Fuck normal. It's time for focus & ferocity, realism & resolve, perspective & priorities. Enough with Kanye's mental disorders. Enough with messages scrawled on the back of the First Lady's coat. Enough with toilet paper stuck to the President's shoe. Enough with all that when we should be saying enough with kids taken from families, enough with white supremacists running a woman over in Charlottesville, enough with old men with four centuries among them blithely dismissing the grace & heroism of a woman recounting before the country her experience of rape by a nominee to the United States Supreme Court. The last four years weren't about normal. They weren't even about abnormal. They weren't about an abnormal President or his abnormal political party that's worse than he is. They're about us. Enough with us? Enough with who we are & what we've become? The long slog toward America v.3 was never going to be settled by a knockout blow or electoral wave, b/c one man was never the enemy. We're the enemy.

Let's ponder a concept strange: Let's cut Donald Trump some slack. This isn't to dispute he's the most malignant American in 150 years. This isn't to dispute his treason, the violence he's inspired against fellow Americans & democracy itself. Rather it's to argue that while it's a prevailing rule among politicians & journalists alike that in a democracy the people are never wrong, that's horseshit. It's not Trump who made America half-stupid — he's not that smart. He's not that charming. Rather it's the America "selfish and proud" that made Trump. The question was never whether Trump was unfit for office, which he himself established beyond anything to which anyone could add. The question is whether the rest of us are fit to be Americans. He's a poor excuse for a man let alone a President, and every moment that we tolerated his presidency, the more we became a poor excuse for a people. Whether we originally selected him for explicitly racist or sexist reasons, at the least we chose to overlook — as sufficient reasons for opposing him — the racism & sexism in which he openly trafficked. We overlooked toxic comments about people of other ethnicities, cultures, religions, genders, orientations, physical challenges. We overlooked mockery of the afflicted, we overlooked his decades of exploiting the poor & dispossessed. We overlooked clear authoritarian impulses & enthusiastic endorsements by the Ku Klux Klan & their fellow travelers. On the world stage we allowed America to be the fat, rich old white guy pushing little countries out of the way to get to the front of the photo op, straightening his tie as he does. So-called progressives who couldn't or wouldn't see the difference between all this & alternatives however imperfect or compromised became their own kind of sociopaths. Trump didn't dishonor us with his election four years ago, we dishonored ourselves. Biden's victory notwithstanding, we must still redeem that dishonor if there's time. Democracy is still at the wall. We're still left to resolve not who he is — we know who he is. We're left to resolve who we are. We're left to resolve the fuliginous rank venom that flows thru some deep blistered vein of our body politic. Long after Trump has departed, his America is still here. It's going to be a long fight lasting years if not decades assuming we haven't already run out of time. If Trump was a President who saw not himself in the context of his country but the country in the context of himself, then we're left to resolve whether we see ourselves in the context of our country or see the country only in the context of our worst selves where no America deserves to exist.

Have I become my own Mark Levin? Maybe I should ground that airplane, the one in my sleep-worn fantasies where I've loaded up the likes of Trump & McConnell? No. Prepare for take-off. Don't bother buckling your seatbelts. Do you think I came all this way & all these words to be edifying? Fuck edifying when you're done fucking normal. Because damned if Levin isn't right. I hate his America b/c I love my America. Damned if Hannity isn't right, damned if Laura Ingraham isn't right, damned if "Judge" Jeanine Pirro isn't right, damned if crazed-gerbil-on-crack Lou Dobbs isn't right, damned if Bow-Tie Tuck the Pot Pie Prince isn't right. In Fox's America proudly I'm a traitor b/c in my America humbly I'm a patriot. Both halves of the country betray each other — we're a nation of traitors & I remain the Patriot of Elsewhere, where my America blasphemes theirs, where my America spits in the face of theirs, where my America is heresy to theirs of the white hood & swinging noose, of the dead stare & false witness borne, of profligate players & the discarded homeless, of the frightened immigrant & native peoples ground to dust, of sweating bullyboys & the are-you-now-or-have-you-ever-been, of auction-block shackles & Black backs latticed with scars, of the Salem stench & the Jesus of "Come to me the little children so I can lock you away in your loveless cage." I hate their America in the name of my America of the eternal pursuit & memory's mystic chord & our natures' better angels & the promise God loves no matter how often we break it. The American civil war goes on. Don't yet lay down your arms.

January 25

As information emerges about the events of Jan 6th, everything that already seemed terrible is revealed to be worse, and the worse it's revealed to be, the more Congressional Republicans assert their cowardice. The Dept of Homeland Security issues a three-month alarm about rising terrorism on the right. Also reported is that two years ago a just-elected Republican member of the House proposed Pelosi be shot and Obama & Hillary be hanged. It's the new President's job to call for unity but presumably he has no more delusions about these people than anyone else should.

On the other hand, here's a headline from several days ago: ANTI-TRUMPERS RECLAIM THE AMERICAN FLAG with a photo of young protesters waving the Stars & Stripes. Yes. This. Now.

January 26

It's not a Dubai penthouse or a flying suite on Emirates, but this afternoon I sign a lease on a flat at the end of Hollywood Blvd off La Brea. A 600-sq-ft space with a window that peers at the Hollywood Hills if I angle the desk just right, it's on the fifth floor of a renovated 96-yr-old deco bldg that used to be headquarters for the Screen Actors Guild & the Oscars when they held their ceremonies a block away at the Roosevelt Hotel. Across the street from the Roosevelt is the Chinese Theater for that day when we can all go to the movies again, and a quarter mile beyond that is Musso & Frank for that day when we all can crowd around their bar again. As I get older, L.A. holds me closer. Some New York director can make a movie about how all aging L.A. novelists live just like this, assuming it crosses the director's mind that anyone actually ever ages in L.A. or, more astonishingly, writes novels. Audrey Hepburn lived in this bldg once as well as the 40th President when he began his career as a film actor. It's a turning of the page that finally feels like my hand is doing the turning rather than someone else's.

January 27

MY RELATIONSHIP WITH THE DIGITAL TOWN square has run its course. Online rumors of my affair with Brontë seem of a piece with other social media altercations — or maybe, per the terms of 21st Century reality, all the other altercations were real too. Brontë is her own kind of survivor, of a leukemia for which doctors once advised she make final arrangements even as, eight yrs later, she remains in this world surely for some reason better than saving my life. *Calm on the out / wild on the in / muse to too many unworthy men...*she might be a song lyric to a melody written by Brian Wilson — *who knows how such rumors begin?* would be the next line — or a legend from a novel. Her father was Preston Sturges's gardener or chauffeur or bookie, I'm still getting the story straight. At the age of 15 she almost lost her virginity to Jimi Hendrix. In other words when she & I finally meet wearing our plague masks like swashbuckling zorro's, it turns out rumors aren't always rumors even when they are. The two of us were just the last to know.

You didn't really believe I made up *hallucinyx*, did you? Who would make up a word like that, and why? Of course it's a real word — I promise. Go ahead, look it up. I wouldn't try to fool you *twice*, would I? It means what I said it means, whatever that was....

January 28

STARING AT HIS "ARCHIVE" THAT HE abandoned 18 months ago, he wonders if the university still wants it. The last 18 months have put a lot in perspective, including him. Naturally he considers just cremating the lot and flinging the ashes to sea like a body. Every now and then it flashes across his mind, "N-N-Nobody's read this yet! Nobody's seen it! I can still get out of this. I can still make a clean getaway, like n-none of it happened!" Maybe he's just being dramatic — he's been known to do that. There's something to be said, nonetheless, for the smoldering of a well-burned bridge over one's shoulder.

January 29

TO MEMORY'S ANOINTED EXECUTIONER, waiting in that doorway at the end of the world: Ready when you are.

STEVE ERICKSON is the author of ten novels — *Days Between Stations, Rubicon Beach, Tours of the Black Clock, Arc d'X, Amnesiascope, The Sea Came in at Midnight, Our Ecstatic Days, Zeroville, These Dreams of You* and *Shadowbahn* — and two books about American politics and popular culture. Numerous editions have been published in English, Spanish, French, German, Italian, Dutch, Polish, Greek, Russian, Chinese and Japanese. Over the years he has written for numerous publications including *Esquire, Rolling Stone, Smithsonian* and the *New York Times Magazine*, and for twelve years he was founding editor of the national literary journal *Black Clock*. Currently he is the film/television critic for *Los Angeles* magazine and a Distinguished Professor at the University of California, Riverside. He has received a Guggenheim fellowship, the American Academy of Arts and Letters Award, and the Lannan Lifetime Achievement Award. In July 2021 the University Press of Mississippi published *Conversations With Steve Erickson* as part of a series that has included Scott Fitzgerald, Ernest Hemingway, William Faulkner, William Burroughs, Gabriel García Márquez and Toni Morrison.